BLAND BUT GRAND
A Cookbook for People on Certain Continuing Diets

BLAND BUT GRAND

A Cookbook for People on Certain Continuing Diets

by Edith M. Peltz

In Cooperation with the Women's Auxiliary
of the Gastro-Intestinal Research Foundation, Inc.

All of the recipes have been tested and approved by the dieti-
cians at the University of Chicago's Billings Hospital.

DOUBLEDAY & COMPANY, INC., GARDEN CITY, NEW YORK

ꙮ FOREWORD

More superstitions relate to food and digestion than to almost any other function of the human body. Nevertheless, more has been learned about food and nutrition in the last fifty years than ever previously. And some of the superstitions have been shown to have a factual basis; not at all based upon the will to believe.

Observations in the laboratory, and at the bedside, have demonstrated that anger, or mental distress, can cause loss of appetite and other digestive symptoms. Thus, many gastrointestinal symptoms can be ascribed to tension, and to anxieties and pressures originating at home or at work. Sometimes a vacation, reassurance, or mild sedation will relieve this type of gastrointestinal difficulty and modification of food intake is neither indicated nor necessary. Allergists often assert that people are sensitive to certain foods and that this sensitivity is manifested by digestive symptoms. When skin tests are made, reactions often are noted to extracts of these foods;

but, unfortunately, skin tests are not the most certain way to establish food allergies. Often the allergy attributed to foods such as chocolate, garlic, and onions cannot be demonstrated conclusively; nevertheless, the individual patient may experience improvement when the suspected food is avoided, whatever the explanation.

Contraversely, medical experience has indicated that some foods may indeed irritate the digestive tract. The irritable digestive tract probably is the most common gastrointestinal disorder for which bland diets are prescribed; and gas, abdominal discomfort, constipation, or diarrhea may be relieved when raw fruits and vegetables, fruit juices, and highly spiced foods are eliminated from the diet, even temporarily. Similar types of diets may be helpful also in the management of inflammatory bowel disease, such as ulcerative colitis or diverticulitis. The elimination of milk sugar (lactose) will relieve completely the flatulence and diarrhea in people with a deficiency of the enzyme lactose. In peptic ulcer, the frequent intake of soft or bland foods is a useful adjunct in the control of the stomach's acid secretion in a patient with an active ulcer. Scientifically, physicians often list the irritating factors as mechanical (fibers and roughage); chemical (foods like vinegar, horseradish, pepper, mustard, pickles, spices, and other condiments); and thermal (excessive hot or cold temperatures). In addition, sweets such as candy, icings, and frostings are concentrated in sugar, and, for reasons not entirely clear, may irritate the lining of the esophagus in patients with esophageal reflux and esophagitis, experienced as "heartburn." Fried foods, greasy foods, and hot bread may produce difficulties for persons with a "weak stomach" or with an irritable digestive tract. Some people complain of gaseous discomfort every time they eat beans, cabbages, onions, green or red peppers, cucumbers, or peanuts; and claim relief when these foods are omitted from the diet. While medical opinions may differ on the significance of this type of information, the more practical approach would appear to be for the person concerned to avoid those foods regarded in his experience as irritating. This often temporary adjustment in food intake usually can be made without imposing a severe dietary burden and without the need to invoke serious psychological consequences.

The goal of the Gastro-Intestinal Research Foundation in Chicago, of which I have been president and chairman of the Board of

Directors, is to help support research in disorders of the digestive tract and particularly to aid Dr. Joseph B. Kirsner of the University of Chicago in directing research in the area of gastrointestinal disease and in training specialists in this field. The purpose of this book is not necessarily to advocate diets in the treatment of digestive disorders; for this is the responsibility of the physician. The objective rather is to suggest useful and palatable food recipes, to assist patients and wives of patients in the preparation of tasty foods, when diets are prescribed for digestive ailments. Almost nothing else is more distressing than facing a meal with a lengthy list of forbidden foods. Usually such lists contain practically everything the person would like to eat. BLAND BUT GRAND offers a way out of such a dilemma, and provides not only many appetizing, tasty, even delightful recipes, but foods and concoctions he will be likely to enjoy without apprehension or distress.

The development of this book has been a special function of the Women's Auxiliary of the Gastro-Intestinal Research Foundation. In its development, Mrs. Howard M. Peltz had the idea and did most of the work. I express here our great appreciation, and my personal admiration for the preparation of a most useful and unique cookbook.

MORRIS FISHBEIN, M.D.

✿ PREFACE

Diets long have been a subject of interest to the physician who seeks all possible assistance in alleviating the symptoms of digestive illness. Diet obviously is a matter of concern to the patient required to forego tasty dishes for "bland" and generally tasteless food, as well as to the patient's wife, who faces the hazard of disapproval because of the traditional monotony of the bland diet. In recent years, diets also have become a matter of scientific controversy, challenged by physicians who are unconvinced of the usefulness of diet regulation in the management of digestive disease.

There is little question that, except perhaps for the gluten-free diet in non-tropical sprue and the salt-free diet for congestive heart failure, diet therapy often rests upon an empirical, subjective basis, whose scientific validity is difficult to establish. And yet, both patients and physicians are aware that, based upon individual experience, diets, though not curative, can be most helpful in the management of patients with peptic ulcer distress or in alleviating the discomfort of patients with the irritable bowel syndrome. And who can debate the practical wisdom of the patient with ulcerative colitis who insists that, scientific evidence notwithstanding, raw fruits and vegetables, and fruit juices, such as orange juice, increase his abdominal pain and diarrhea. Diets, indeed, can be useful adjuncts in the management of gastrointestinal illness. The bland diet, despite its shortcomings, relieves abdominal discomfort and helps to regulate bowel function, when applied with intelligence and discretion.

The author of this book, BLAND BUT GRAND, has performed a most important service to the medical profession and to the many patients who must observe dietary restrictions. Many useful and tasty recipes have been collected, reflecting initiative, imagination, and ingenuity, often lacking in routine dietary programs. This compendium, indeed, is a fine collection of recipes which should provide many happy eating experiences for the patient on a bland diet. It is not beyond the stretch of imagination to predict the popularity of these culinary delights even among those who are not required to observe a diet. The variety of tasty recipes presented here may very well render obsolete present differences of opinion between erstwhile opponents and longtime advocates of the bland diet. My congratulations to Mrs. Howard M. Peltz for this valuable effort.

JOSEPH B. KIRSNER, M.D., *Professor Medicine*
Department of Medicine, University of Chicago

🌿 CONTENTS

Recipes for items followed by an asterisk may be located by consulting the Index.

🌺 INTRODUCTION

The recipes in this book are your "G.I." Bill of Rights (*G*astro-*In*testinal), a guarantee for the privilege of your pursuit of tasty, tempting, tried and tested formulas for BLAND BUT GRAND food.

Freedom of variety!

Freedom of delicious flavoring!

Freedom of substitutes for restricted ingredients!

Freedom of using the most ingenious recipes your imagination, your appetite, and your doctor could desire!

Freedom of enjoying meals that have been planned with devotion and care!

Freedom of approval by the dietician at Billings Hospital, University of Chicago!

THESE FREEDOMS ARE YOURS!

Sharpen your appetite! BLAND BUT GRAND recipes will make you feel like a gourmet!

In compiling this cookbook, I have hoped to help not only the numerous people on restricted diets, but also the cook who, in many instances, is finding it difficult to have variety in the diet menus. This can very easily not only make the person on the diet dread mealtime but it may also make him constantly aware of his condition and envelop him with self-pity over his sad plight.

The housewife, cooking for the husband or child on the diet, becomes more harried and irritable because the patient takes no pleasure in her cooking and she has the added task of preparing two separate meals constantly because she cannot subject the rest of the family to the limited diet of the patient.

I feel that the majority of these recipes can be used for the entire family, as I have done my utmost to make them as flavorful as possible. This should enable the housewife, at least several times a week, to prepare only one meal, and the patient should not only feel less of a burden but, I trust, get greater enjoyment out of an enlarged variety . . . variety being the only "spice" included in this book.

"EATIQUETTE"

or *How to accept a dinner invitation without cheating on your diet*

When invited to someone's home for dinner, don't take a chance on what will be served; some hostesses smother even a roast with onions and garlic.

When invited by someone who does not know about your diet, without going into great details about your condition, politely ask if you may come over after dinner as you are on a diet and don't wish to inconvenience her. She may say that would be fine but, most likely, she will insist you come for dinner and she will gladly prepare something you can eat. At this point you could ask what she is serving as most of the meal might be acceptable. If it isn't, most hostesses would not find it difficult to broil a few hamburgers or a steak. It is, of course, up to you to inform her that you are allowed no seasoning, except salt.

If a hostess ever feels upset because you have to skip her prize culinary accomplishment, just remember, if you eat it, she may be a great deal more upset when she comes to visit you in the hospital.

To members of the family, or friends who may invite you frequently . . . why not give them a copy of this book?

"WHEN WITH THEM YOU SUP, THEY CAN LOOK IT UP."

"TRICKS FOR TREATS"

READ LABELS on packaged foods to check ingredients. Even items like tomato juice should be checked as some brands add spices. Many canned baby foods contain onions.

Be cautious when buying cakes in a bakery as many include nuts. Pre-packaged cakes are safer as they list ingredients.

DON'T ASSUME that all restaurants broil hamburgers; many of them grill or fry but most can broil on request.

When eating hamburgers out, you have, undoubtedly, discovered that many restaurants now carry only hamburger rolls with sesame seeds. Ask if they have a plain Kaiser roll, plain hot dog bun, or white bread or, if need be, ask for two bottoms of the buns that they have as the bottoms generally only have a few seeds, which can be easily removed.

NO CRUSTS should form on foods such as casseroles.

STEAKS should not be eaten rare as fibers are not broken down sufficiently; nor should they be too well done as a crust forms which makes it less digestible. "Aim for a happy medium."

 # DIET CODE

and General Information

This book in no way intends to prescribe a diet for the various gastrointestinal diseases. These recipes are intended for people on continuing diets and not applicable to acute or post-operative situations. The diet for each disease will vary, based on the individual's own condition, and it is *strongly* urged that the patient does not deviate from the diet prescribed to him by his physician.

A simple code has been used, which precedes each recipe. A diet number is used to identify those recipes that pertain to particular groupings of illnesses. In many instances technical and nontechnical synonyms have been used for the diseases covered because many diseases are known by more than one name.

The code, using numbers 1 through 3, represents the following:

Diet 1   *Ulcer*—which includes:
   Peptic Ulcer
   Ulcer of the Stomach
   Ulcer of the Duodenum

Diet 2   (a) *Irritable Digestive Tract*—which includes:
   Spastic Colon
   Mucous Colitis
   Spastic Constipation

   (b) *Inflammatory Bowel Disease*—which includes:
   Ulcerative Colitis
   Regional Ileitis
   Regional Enteritis
   Ileocolitis
   Granulomatous Colitis
   Proctitis
   Crohn's Disease

   (c) *Diverticulitis*

Diet 3   *Gluten-free Diet*—which includes:
   Malabsorption
   Non-tropical Sprue
   Steatorrhea
   Fatty Diarrhea

Those patients who find their disease listed under either 2a, 2b, or 2c may make use of those recipes that include the number 2 after the word DIET which precedes the recipe.

I must stress that should a recipe recommended for any of the diets include an ingredient that the patient's own physician has advised him to avoid, *please avoid the recipe* as your tolerance to certain food items may vary from that of other patients with your illness. Where this book must deal in generalities regarding these diets, your doctor deals with you as an individual and can, therefore, be very specific regarding your condition.

There are some pieces of information that I would like to pass on as, in speaking to numerous people on diets, or those cooking for someone on a diet, it came to my attention that certain valuable and important facts concerning these diets were, unfortunately, unknown to them.

In many instances this was the typical case where the wife or mother of a patient was familiar with the diet only to the extent of the printed list of allowed foods that the patient in her family was given by the doctor. In some instances, parts of the diet presented questions but, hesitating to bother the doctor, she was prone to rely on her own judgment and, in many instances, erred.

As spices are not allowed on any of the diets covered, many of the recipes derive their flavor from wine, which could hardly be considered a poor substitute. Wine, as a beverage, is, of course, taboo on these diets; however, when wine is used in cooking and is allowed to boil for several minutes, the alcohol evaporates, leaving only a pleasant flavoring agent.

While on this subject, many people have an erroneous idea regarding another agent, namely, the onion. Homemade chicken soup is extremely popular, it seems, with most people on these diets, and the average cook takes extreme pride in her particular recipe for this soup, which, of course, calls for onions. The cooks are well aware that onion is taboo but, since they feel chicken soup isn't chicken soup without it and they take care in removing the whole onion after the soup has been cooked, they feel they are following the diet carefully. This is somewhat of a fallacy. Though eating a whole onion, or pieces of it, may be distressing, the residue of the onion that was cooked with the soup . . . and there is residue because the soup retains the onion flavor . . . can also be distressing.

In addition to observing the diet, and by diet this means not only limiting yourself to the allowed foods but also adhering to the prescribed process of preparation which excludes any form of frying. It is also recommended that extra care be given to avoid food spoilage.

Food should not be left out of the refrigerator any longer than necessary and this also applies to freshly cooked food. If food that has just been cooked is allowed to cool completely before it is refrigerated, you may save a few pennies on your electric bill but you may also be refrigerating the bacteria that you have allowed to form on the food while it was sitting out. Let the hot food cool just slightly and then refrigerate.

The average housewife today, like a good businessman, has learned not only to be a good shopper but also to be a thrifty one. She has, in addition, learned how to utilize leftover food so that nothing is wasted. Though this is admirable and, in many instances, a necessity, it can be harmful thrift.

Certain foods begin to perish before they acquire a bad taste or smell or show an indication of mold. If the food has been around for some time, a good motto is "WHEN IN DOUBT, THROW IT OUT." With an item like bacon, for example, it may prove cheaper to buy a small quantity for your immediate needs than to purchase the larger economical package and end up throwing out the unused portion because it is no longer fresh.

Most of you understand the difference between the various types of freezers but, unfortunately, there are still many people who do not and without going into an extensive discussion on this topic, I only wish to alert everyone to the fact that these differences exist. There are books out on this subject, magazines and newspapers periodically carry features on this topic, and, if you have a specific question concerning your particular refrigerator or freezer, contact the manufacturer of your particular model. They are usually most cooperative and, of course, the best equipped to help you. "WHEN IN DOUBT, FIND OUT."

I just wish to point out that there are three basic types of freezers which may differ greatly as to the length of storage time recommended. The three types are deep freezer storage chest, double outer door refrigerator, and single door refrigerator with freezer compartment.

Finally, though very important, the patient must acquire a mature outlook to the overall diet picture. He is, after all, the one subjected to the diet and must, within himself, learn the self-discipline required to abstain from many foods he has previously enjoyed.

Once he has reconciled himself to the fact that if he cheats, he cheats only himself, and is willing to adhere only to the prescribed foods, the next step may be simpler.

All of us, whether on diets or not, undoubtedly dislike, or are indifferent to, certain foods. If we have no restrictions on our diet, we can afford to pamper our taste buds pretty much and eat only what we enjoy.

When that vast choice of foods is narrowed down considerably, as it is in the diets we are covering, and the patient, in looking at the list of allowed items, decides he never liked 50 percent of these items before he was on the diet and will not eat them now, isn't he really making the diet harder on himself than it need be?

Most of us would never have eaten that second green olive based on our initial reaction if we had not been told that it was one of those foods for which you must acquire a taste.

Did you ever see people take a caviar appetizer while they are telling you they really don't like it but they are trying to acquire a taste for it because it is considered a delicacy? If the patient will now try to acquire a taste for some of the things he wouldn't eat before, he may find his diet isn't really so limited after all.

Some people consider a good casserole a delicacy. Men generally don't like them. Perhaps their dislike stems from eating one casserole and, perhaps, that one really wasn't a delicacy. If they are among the people who hated the taste of the first olive but eventually cultivated a taste for them, at least they should give a few more casseroles, and themselves, a chance.

I have tried, in this book, to give the patient interesting recipes, but they can only fulfill that aim if the patient will cooperate and show a willingness to experiment with foods previously not eaten but allowed on his diet and by utilizing a little imagination.

You are urged always to read your recipes well in advance of preparation time, preferably the day before. This is not only to assure you of having all the ingredients available but, in many instances, a good portion of a recipe, or the entire recipe, may be made in advance of the final cooking process.

It has taken quite a long time to compile these relatively few recipes and, though it may seem difficult for the reader to believe, I feel certain that by taking additional time, this quantity could easily be doubled or tripled. However, based on the reaction of the people who have known that this book was in work, and their urgent desire to obtain a copy of the finished product as quickly as possible, it is felt that the recipes herein might stimulate the reader's imagination to such a point that additional recipes could be created easily by the cook who will experiment a little.

FOREWORD

from a Patient

In the fall of 1958, when I was thirty years old, I was told by my doctor, after enduring three months of abdominal disturbance, to go on a bland diet and to take some tests to determine the source of my trouble.

I took the tests, but at that time no one could have convinced me that many of the foods that I had been eating, and equating with health, were now harmful to me. So I went on eating what I pleased.

Soon after that I was hospitalized for an inflammatory bowel disease.

I had extreme pain, and was completely unable to take food, which caused me a considerable loss of weight.

After making some progress I was sent home and ordered to remain on a bland diet. At first I feared and distrusted food; I soon became indifferent. I still wasn't feeling very well and with my attitude toward food it was easy to stay on a bland diet. I couldn't have cared less whether I ate or not.

It wasn't until my state of health progressed further and I had begun to take an interest in food again that the diet bothered me. I had finally convinced myself that the diet was important and was determined to follow it strictly.

I had a printed diet and a narrowly drawn list of permissible foods given to me by my doctor. Like so many others on similar diets I fell into a routine of eating broiled steaks and chops most of the time. My appetite continued but I was beginning to tire of the lack of variety. Eating was becoming a very frustrating experience.

By now I was back at work and socializing again. It became a toss-up as to which was more traumatic, eating lunch in restaurants during the day or being invited to dinner parties at night.

There was the inevitable explanation to chefs, short-order cooks, Chinese waiters, and well-intending hostesses: "I cannot eat this and I cannot eat that and couldn't you possibly substitute something else?" There were times when the menu was so impossible for me that I was glad to make a meal out of bread without seeds (which is surprisingly not always that easy to find when you are eating out).

I was not one to be complacent about the state of things. I sought more information from doctors about my diet; I read a great deal. As I became more knowledgeable I found it was much easier to adjust to the diet. I became defensive about my health and learned to cope with restaurant help and hostesses. I found that if you are tactful but firm most restaurants will substitute items or specially prepare dishes for you, leaving out harmful ingredients.

By 1960 when I married I was feeling well and was able to liberalize my diet with doctor's permission. My new bride knew of my bowel disease before we were married but could not fully appreciate its seriousness because I was doing so well at the time I met her.

But, the flare-ups eventually came and after a few visits to the hospital, my wife became very concerned. She had lived with me and my condition several years now and understood it as well as I did. She was determined to do all she could to keep me well. In the area of diet, she groped for answers to questions and sought advice from doctors and dieticians. She wanted to follow my diet as strictly as possible and yet give me the greatest choice of food.

At various times I was on extremely high doses of steroids, which greatly increased my appetite. This gave my wife the two-fold task of satisfying my abnormally large appetite while on steroids and stimulating my diminished appetite when I was off or low on the drug.

What the diet-ridden individual needs most is substitutes that resemble the types of foods he used to eat. He may not have had spareribs with barbecue sauce for years but he nostalgically remembers their taste. He longs for them. Now, if you can create a dish that resembles a former favorite food, without using ingredients that are taboo, his former memories will dominate his present mental reaction to taste. If he is an imaginative person, he will sustain as much satisfaction from the harmless substitute as he did from his former favorite dish.

My wife was able to recognize this principle of substitution. At first, creating new recipes was difficult, but, each new dish or sauce would give her ideas for further creations. A few recipes snowballed into a great many.

This book contains most of the recipes created by my wife and collected from others over a period of years. In a way it was a joint effort, she cooked and I ate. . . . I was never a fussy eater and I had a willingness to try new things. This is an important attitude for the patient to develop.

Both of us hope that this book will spare the reader from the trial and error period that we went through.

HOWARD M. PELTZ

🌿 APPETIZERS

The role of the hostess, always an important one, takes on two added tasks when dealing with a guest on a diet, or, dealing with guests who are not on diets and a member of her family who is.

One is to prepare proper foods for the diet patient and the other is to be thoughtful of his possible sensitivity to his condition. With a little foresight, these added tasks are really quite simple.

The hostess should always have at least one of the diet appetizers available for the patient or she could make several of the diet recipes and cut down on the others. After all, the BLAND BUT GRAND recipes can't hurt anyone who is not on a diet and you needn't advertise them as being bland. Some of our guests, to our pleasure and amusement, have cleaned us out of the Tuna Log and left us with the spicier tidbits.

I suggest that the thoughtful hostess take the diet patient aside and tell him which appetizers have been prepared with his diet in mind. It is, after all, the patient's prerogative to decide whether he cares to mention his diet, which will lead to questions about his illness.

I might add that if it is the hostess herself who is on the diet, she should most certainly make an appetizer she can eat. There is no reason to play the martyr and her guests will feel most uncomfortable if they see she has fussed to make delicacies, none of which she can enjoy.

A good hostess should, after all, enjoy her own party.

Diet: 1–2

CHEESE BALLS

2 tablespoons sour cream
Ritz cracker crumbs

1 package (3 ounces) cream cheese
2 slices American cheese

Heat and stir all ingredients, except crumbs, in a saucepan over low heat, until American cheese is completely dissolved and can be blended smoothly with other ingredients.

Refrigerate for about 5 hours.

To make crumbs, place about 20 crackers in a plastic food bag, secure tightly, break the crackers up a little with hands and then use a rolling pin. Pour crumbs on a flat surface.

When cheese mixture has been refrigerated for 5 hours, use a melon scoop to scoop out the cheese mixture. Roll in hands to form balls and then roll in cracker crumbs.

Refrigerate until ready to serve.

Makes 6 to 8 balls.

Diet: 1–2–3[1]

CHEESE SPREAD OR DIP

1 package (3 ounces) cream cheese
2 tablespoons sour cream
2 slices American cheese

Heat and stir all ingredients in saucepan, over low heat, until American cheese is completely dissolved and can be blended smoothly with other ingredients.

When slightly cooled, pour into a jar with a tight lid and refrigerate.

May be used as a dip for 3 or 4 people or spread on crackers or bread.[1]

[1] Diet 3 can use this spread but, of course, only on gluten-free items.

Diet: 1–2

CHEESE STRAWS

1 cup flour   *¼ pound grated American*
Pinch salt   *cheese*
½ cup butter, creamed   *2½ tablespoons milk*

Preheat oven to 350° F. Sift flour with salt and blend into butter. Add cheese and milk to make a stiff dough. Roll thin on lightly floured surface. Cut into sticks and bake for 10 minutes.

Serve warm.

Makes about 24 straws.

Diet: 1–2

HOT CHEESE CRACKER CRUNCHIES

1 package (3 ounces) cream   *1 pinch baking powder*
   cheese   *10–12 Ritz crackers*
1 egg yolk

Allow cream cheese to soften, then mash with fork. Add yolk and baking powder and mix well. Cover top of each cracker with mixture and place under broiler for about 2 minutes. Serve immediately.
Makes 10 to 12 appetizers.

Diet: 1–2–3[2]

CHICKEN-LIVER PATE

½ pound chicken livers   *1 tablespoon finely chopped*
2 eggs, hard-cooked   *canned green beans*
2 packages (3-ounce size)   *¾ teaspoon salt*
   cream cheese

Drop chicken livers into boiling salted water and simmer until barely done but tender.
Mix livers and eggs through food grinder (or put in blender, a little at a time; blend, covered, at high speed). If no grinder or blender is available, mash ingredients together until proper consistency is achieved.
With wooden spoon, work cream cheese until light and fluffy. Mix cheese into liver mixture along with remaining ingredients.
Serve with hot toast or crackers.[2]
Makes 1½ cups.

[2] Diet 3 must use this with gluten-free item.

Diet: 1-2-3[3]

TUNA LOG

1 package (8 ounces) soft
cream cheese
1 can (7 ounces) tuna,
drained and flaked
1 or 2 teaspoons Homemade
*Barbecue Sauce**

¼ teaspoon salt
¼ cup very finely chopped
canned French-style green
beans

Combine cream cheese, tuna, barbecue sauce, salt, and about 2 tablespoons of the chopped green beans. (Add the barbecue sauce a little at a time and adjust to personal taste.) Shape into a roll about 1½ inches in diameter.

Sprinkle remaining chopped green beans on a sheet of waxed paper. Roll cheese roll in chopped beans; wrap in waxed paper and chill in refrigerator for several hours before serving.

Place on a long tray and serve with crackers.[3]

Serves 6 to 10.

It's amusing to note how the guests who are not on diets will abandon their spicy appetizers for this tuna log, fighting the "diet" guests for this "bland" spread. Keep them guessing as to the ingredients for a while because they invariably insist it's too tasty to be acceptable for bland diets.

[3] Diet 3 must use this with gluten-free item.

 # SOUPS

The soup recipes are few but here is where personal preferences and a little imagination will greatly expand the category.

The Cream of Chicken Soup is really the base of so many soups that it is left up to the reader to try the art of experimental cooking.

You are in the best position to decide if your patient would prefer your adding rice instead of noodles or peas instead of carrots or, perhaps, both. A little of the cooked chicken, cut up and added to the soup, will certainly never hurt.

Though I recommend following instructions when you
bake a cake
While cooking soup......................try to create

Diet: 2–3

BEEF TEA

> *1 pound top round steak*
> *2 cups cold water*
> *¼ to ½ teaspoon salt*

Cut meat into small pieces, about ½ inch cubes, and let stand in the cold water for 2 hours, in refrigerator. (This may be done right in the pot it is to be cooked in.)

Bring to a boil and then reduce heat to very low and just barely simmer for 2 hours. Adjust flavor by adding more salt.

Serve in a cup with the bits of meat.

Makes 2 cups.

Diet: 2–3

CREAM OF CHICKEN SOUP

> *4 tablespoons butter or*
> *chicken fat*
> *4 tablespoons flour (or 2*
> *tablespoons cornstarch for*
> *Diet 3)*
>
> *4 cups chicken broth—*
> *homemade or canned*[1]
> *1 cup light cream*
> *1 teaspoon salt*

Over direct heat, melt butter in top of a double boiler. Add flour (or cornstarch) and cook for 2 minutes, stirring constantly. Remove pan from heat and add chicken broth slowly, stirring constantly. Return to heat and bring just to a boil, stirring constantly. Place over boiling water and add the cream. Taste and add salt, if needed.

Serves 4 to 6.

[1] Of the canned soups I tried, the only ones I have found that contain no spices or onions are the Richelieu and Monarch brands of clear chicken broth.

Diet: 1–2

EGG BARLEY CHICKEN SOUP WITH PEAS

8 chicken wings
1 quart cold water
1 tablespoon salt
1 carrot, diced
1 can (8½ ounces) young
small peas, not drained

1 cup water
½ teaspoon salt
2 tablespoons egg barley

Clean wings and place in soup kettle with water and salt. Bring to boiling point slowly. Cover with tight lid and simmer for 1 hour. Add diced carrot and can of peas, with liquid, and continue simmering for ½ hour longer.

Bring 1 cup water and ½ teaspoon salt to boil. Add the egg barley and continue boiling for 10 minutes. Put barley in a strainer, rinse with cold water, and add to soup. Simmer for a few minutes until ready to serve.

Serves 4.

🪷 MEATS

In this chapter on meats, the preparation of plain steaks, chops, and roasts has been omitted because the patient has, undoubtedly, been living on these. Should you initially open this book to a recipe for a steak that is merely put in the broiler you would, justifiably, have great doubts about the originality of this book.

I feel these meat dishes offer quite a variety. The average housewife who enjoys cooking and has no diet to contend with generally relies on a variety of meals no greater than the variety offered herein and only on occasion will she try something really new and different.

A number of people, not on diets, who have eaten the Breaded Veal Cutlets, which are baked, enjoyed them so much they no longer prepare theirs any other way. Here again, a little imagination can give you another recipe. Why not pour tomato sauce (naturally this means tomato juice that has been thickened with cornstarch) over the veal cutlets and, if you are not on the Gluten-free Diet, serve them with buttered spaghetti, just like in Italian restaurants.

Hopefully you will find that many items that you previously pan-fried are far easier, and less messy, to prepare in the oven and far healthier for the other members of the family who have no gastrointestinal disorders.

The Beef Stew is also very popular in many non-diet households. Again, there is no messy skillet to wash. It takes practically no time to combine all the ingredients in the casserole. You can do it in the morning, refrigerate it, and just put it in the oven 3 hours before it's time to eat.

Regarding the Barbecued Beef Spareribs, I can only say that I hope your patient is as excited the first time you prepare them as my guinea pig patient was.

If your patient has even the slightest imagination, when you place the casserole of Mock Beef Imperial in front of him, he will think you forgot his diet because it looks like there are slices of onions in it. Even the texture is similar . . . it's amazing what happens to those julienne-cut beets when you cook them.

Diet: 1–2–3

FLANK STEAK, ROSE

1 flank steak, about 1½   1 teaspoon salt
   pounds   Oil for brushing meat
¾ cup dry rosé wine   (optional)

Place meat in medium-sized bowl. Combine wine and salt and pour over meat. Cover and marinate in refrigerator at least 2 hours, turning meat several times. Drain and save marinade.

Brush meat with oil (optional) and broil to medium rare or medium.

Cut thin slices by cutting diagonally across grain of meat.

The marinade may be used as a sauce by adding 1 or 2 tablespoons butter to the marinade, bringing the mixture to a boil, and spooning it over the meat.

Serves 5 or 6.

Diet: 1–2

MOCK BEEF IMPERIAL

1 pound boneless beef cut
into 1-inch cubes
1 can (1 pound) julienne-cut
beets and 1 cup beet juice[1]
3 tablespoons Home
Barbecue Sauce*
1 jar (2½ ounces) mushrooms,
chopped very fine, and
mushroom juice, if necessary

½ cup instant flour
1 teaspoon salt
1 or 2 teaspoons soy sauce
(optional)
Egg Biscuit Topping

Preheat oven to 350° F.

Combine all ingredients, except topping, in a 2-quart casserole. Cover and bake for ½ hour. Stir thoroughly, cover again, and bake for about 1 hour more, or until meat is tender.

Drop topping by spoonfuls onto meat mixture. Bake about 20 minutes longer.

Serves 6.

[1] If can of beets does not yield 1 cup juice, make up difference with mushroom juice.

Egg Biscuit Topping

1 cup water
Chunk butter
½ teaspoon salt
½ cup milk

1½ cups mashed potato flakes
1 egg
¼ cup instant flour

Heat water, butter, and salt to boiling in saucepan. Remove from heat and add milk. Stir in potato flakes. When flakes are soft and moist, whip lightly with fork. Add egg and flour. Blend well and drop by spoonfuls over meat.

Diet: 1–2–3

LEFTOVER LOAF

Preheat oven to 350° F.

Line a well-buttered bread pan, bottom and sides, with an inch of salted mashed potatoes.

Chop together any leftover cooked vegetables and meat (as allowed on diet). Add salt, mix together with a beaten egg and a little gravy, and fill the loaf pan.

Put mashed potatoes on top and bake until brown.

If pan was well greased, loaf should slip out easily.

Number of portions will, of course, depend on amount of leftovers used.

Diet: 1–2–3

BEEF SPARERIBS

3 to 4 ribs per person (about 1 pound)

Separate the ribs and marinate in dry red wine to cover for about 1 hour.

Preheat oven to 350° F.

Place ribs on rack placed over pan to hold drippings. A cookie sheet, lined with foil, works well.

Bake for about 1 hour, or until tender.

Diet: 1–2–3

BARBECUED BEEF SPARERIBS

2 pounds beef spareribs, separated
Homemade Barbecue Sauce

Preheat oven to 400° F.
Place individual ribs, curved side down, on rack in shallow pan.
(Line pan with aluminum foil for easier cleaning.) Brush ribs, on both
sides, with sauce and bake for 15 minutes. Then reduce heat to
325° F. and bake 1½ hours, or until ribs are tender, brushing ribs
on both sides with additional sauce every half hour. If desired, any
remaining sauce may be served in a bowl or poured over ribs.
Serves 2.

Homemade Barbecue Sauce

2 teaspoons Sanka instant
coffee
½ cup boiling water
½ cup tomato juice

2 teaspoons cornstarch
½ teaspoon salt
2 tablespoons burgundy wine
¼ cup sugar

Combine all ingredients, dissolving coffee in hot water and gradually stirring tomato juice into cornstarch before adding to other ingredients. Simmer for 10 minutes, stirring frequently. Let cool slightly
before brushing on ribs.

Diet: 2–3

BEEF STEW

*1 pound stewing meat, cut
into bite-size pieces (a cut
called "Scotch Tender" is
excellent, as is sirloin)
1 can (8½ ounces) small
peas, and liquid
1 can (8 ounces) tomato
juice (make certain brand
used has only salt added)*

*½ cup cleaned and sliced
carrots
2 medium potatoes, peeled
and cut into large pieces
1 teaspoon salt
1 to 2 tablespoons water
1 tablespoon cornstarch*

Preheat oven to 350° F.

Mix all ingredients, except cornstarch and water, in a 2-quart casserole with tight lid and place in oven for 2½ hours.

In a small saucepan, mix 1 to 2 tablespoons cold water with the cornstarch and, when smooth, slowly stir in about a half cup of hot liquid from stew.

Pour cornstarch mixture into stew and mix well. Return to oven for an additional half hour.

Makes 3 to 4 servings.

Note: If using a less tender cut of meat than those suggested, slightly more liquid will be required.

Diet: 1–2

BAKED BURGERS

1½ pounds ground beef
⅔ cup evaporated milk
½ cup fine cracker meal
1 egg
1½ teaspoons salt

2 cups grated American
  cheese
American cheese strips
1 loaf French bread

Preheat oven to 350° F.

Combine all ingredients, except cheese and French bread, in a large mixing bowl and mix thoroughly. Add grated cheese and mix lightly.

Cut the loaf of bread in half lengthwise. Spread meat mixture over cut surface of halves. Wrap foil around crust of each half, leaving top uncovered. Bake on cookie sheet in oven for 25 minutes.

Garnish with cheese strips and bake an additional 5 minutes.

Makes 4 to 6 servings.

Diet: 1–2–3

BURGUNDY BURGERS   *Not so hot*

1 pound lean ground beef
¼ cup burgundy, or other
  dry red dinner wine

1 teaspoon salt
Burgundy Sauce

Combine beef, wine, and salt and mix lightly with fork. Shape into 3 or 4 patties. Broil until done as desired. Spoon burgundy sauce over each.

Serves 2 or 3.

Burgundy Sauce

2 tablespoons butter
2 tablespoons soy sauce
2 tablespoons finely chopped
  green beans

3 tablespoons burgundy, or
  other dry red wine

Heat together all ingredients. This may be thickened slightly with a small amount of cornstarch mixed with cold water, or it may be left thin. Spoon over meat.

Diet: 1–2–3

HONEY OF A HAMBURGER

1 pound ground beef
¾ teaspoon salt
2 tablespoons heavy cream (or
  half and half)

Honey

Preheat broiler.
Work meat lightly with hands and add salt and cream. Shape loosely into 5 cakes about 1 inch thick.
Place patties on a rack that fits over drip pan and brush each patty generously with honey.
Place under broiler. When brown, turn and brush exposed side generously with honey and finish broiling.
Serves 2 to 3.

Diet: 1–2

CHEESEBURGER MEAT LOAF

1½ pounds ground beef	*¼ pound American cheese,*
1 small can (5⅓ ounces)	*grated*
evaporated milk	*2 to 3 teaspoons Homemade*
½ cup bread crumbs	*Barbecue Sauce**
1 egg	*½ cup grated American*
1½ teaspoons salt	*cheese*

Preheat oven to 350° F.

Mix together beef, milk, crumbs, egg, and salt. Place half of meat mixture in 9×5×3-inch pan.

Combine ¼ pound grated cheese and barbecue sauce. Spread over meat mixture in pan and top with remaining meat. Bake for 1 hour.

Just before serving, sprinkle with additional cheese and return to oven, or place under broiler, until cheese melts.

Makes 6 servings.

Diet: 1–2

CHOPPED BEEF RING

2 pounds ground beef	*4 slices white bread*
¼ cup butter (optional), if	*1½ teaspoons salt*
desired for flavor	*⅔ cup tomato juice*
½ cup very finely chopped	*⅓ cup Homemade Catsup*
canned green beans	

Mix together beef, butter, chopped green beans, bread (broken into small pieces), and salt.

Preheat oven to 450° F.

Mix thoroughly and moisten with ⅔ cup tomato juice. Pack mixture into a generously buttered ring mold. Spread tomato catsup over the top of the mixture and bake ring for 45 minutes, or until the top is delicately brown and the meat shrinks from the sides of the mold.

Unmold on a heated platter and fill center with vegetables, preferably creamed, or creamed mushrooms, if allowed.

Serves 6.

Homemade Catsup

1 teaspoon cornstarch	*1 tablespoon burgundy wine*
½ cup tomato juice	*¼ teaspoon salt*
1 teaspoon sugar	

Place cornstarch in saucepan and gradually stir in tomato juice, making smooth paste. Add other ingredients, stirring until mixture comes to a boil. Simmer for 10 minutes and remove from heat. Cool slightly and refrigerate in jar with tight cover.

Yield: ½ cup.

Diet: 1–2

HAMBURGER AND POTATO ROLL

2 slices bread (preferably egg bread), top crust removed	*2 tablespoons dry bread crumbs*
1 pound ground beef	*2 cups salted mashed potatoes (hot)*
1 teaspoon salt	*3 slices bacon or beef fry*
1 egg	

Preheat oven to 350° F.

Soften bread in water. Press out excess water and add to ground beef. Mix thoroughly with salt and egg.

Sprinkle a piece of waxed paper with bread crumbs. Press meat out on crumbs to make a rectangle about ½ inch thick. Whip mashed potatoes and spread on top of meat. Potatoes must be hot or they will not spread properly. (If using leftover potatoes, reheat in double boiler before spreading.)

Using waxed paper to help, roll meat and potatoes, jelly-roll fashion, and place in a shallow pan (a pie pan will do).

If meat is very lean, grease pan first. Place bacon or beef fry on top and baste at least once during baking. Bake about 1 hour. Serves 4.

Note: This can be put together earlier in the day, covered, and refrigerated until time to put in oven. It is preferable to remove from refrigerator about 15 or 20 minutes before actually placing in oven.

Suggestion: Serve with sauce, such as the one used for chicken livers, Rich Brown Sauce*, or the Homemade Barbecue Sauce*.

Diet: 1–2

MEAT LOAF

1½ pounds ground beef   *1 egg, beaten*
¾ cup bread crumbs   *1 cup tomato juice—make*
1½ teaspoons salt   *sure brand is bland*

Preheat oven to 350° F.

Combine all ingredients thoroughly and pack firmly into a 9×5×3-inch loaf pan.

Bake about 1½ hours. Let stand 5 minutes before slicing. Makes 8 servings.

Diet: 1–2–3   *Good*

"PORCUPINES"
—GROUND BEEF AND RICE BALLS

4 cups tomato juice[2]	*1 pound lean ground beef*
1 teaspoon brown sugar	*½ cup uncooked rice*
3 tablespoons burgundy wine	*1 egg, beaten*
Pinch baking soda	*1½ teaspoons salt*

Preheat oven to 350° F.

Combine tomato juice, brown sugar, wine, and baking soda in a saucepan. Cover and simmer sauce for 10 minutes.

Meanwhile, combine meat, rice, egg, and salt and mix well. Form into 1½-inch balls. Place in a baking dish. Pour tomato sauce over balls. Cover and bake for 1 hour.

Makes 6 servings.

Note: If you have any meatballs and sauce left over, mash meatballs in sauce, reheat in oven or on top of stove, and use, for example, as a sauce over spaghetti. This would not, of course, apply to Diet 3.

[2] Make sure you check label on tomato juice and pick a brand that has only salt added.

Diet: 1–2

BREADED VEAL CUTLETS

2 tablespoons dry sauterne wine	*2 cups Rice Krispies crumbs*
1 egg, beaten	*3 to 4 tablespoons butter or margarine, melted*
2 thin veal steaks	

Stir wine into beaten egg and marinate veal steaks in this mixture, in refrigerator, for at least 1 hour.

Preheat oven to 350° F.

Make crumbs out of Rice Krispies by putting them in a plastic bag, closing top, and going over bag with a rolling pin.

Pour crumbs on plate and press both sides of veal steaks in crumbs so that meat is heavily coated.

Place meat in large, shallow, greased Pyrex, or other type oven-proof baking dish. Pat any remaining crumbs on tops of steaks. Brush melted butter on tops of steaks very generously. Quantity of butter needed will vary slightly depending on size of steaks.

Bake for approximately 35 to 40 minutes, or until meat is tender and crumbs slightly brown. Do not turn meat.

Serves 2.

Diet: 1–2

GOURMET VEAL LOAF

*1½ pounds ground veal
    shoulder meat*
2 cups grated raw carrots
*1 jar (2½ ounces)
    mushrooms, drained and
    finely chopped*
*½ cup canned, drained, and
    finely chopped French-style
    green beans*

*½ cup very fine Rice Krispies
    crumbs (bread crumbs
    may be used)*
1 teaspoon salt
*2 tablespoons dry sauterne
    wine*
1 cup sour cream

Preheat oven to 350° F.

Combine all ingredients in large bowl and mix lightly with fork. Spoon into loaf pan that measures 9×5×3. Invert into shallow baking pan. Carefully remove loaf pan and score top of loaf lightly.

Bake about 1½ hours or until rich golden brown on top.

Serves 4.

Diet: 2–3[3]

VEAL A LA KING IN NOODLE RING[3]

Noodle Ring[3]

2 tablespoons soft butter or
margarine
1 package (6 ounces)
medium noodles
1 tablespoon butter or
margarine, melted

3 eggs
¾ cup milk
½ teaspoon salt
1 tablespoon finely chopped
canned, French-style green
beans (optional)

Preheat oven to 350° F.

Make noodle ring. Using the soft butter, generously grease a 5½-cup ring mold.

Cook noodles as package label directs; drain. Toss with the melted butter.

Beat eggs with milk, salt, and green beans until just combined. Add to hot noodles, tossing lightly.

Turn noodle mixture into prepared ring mold. Set in pan containing 1 inch hot water and bake, uncovered, for 40 minutes, or just until knife, inserted 1 inch from edge, comes out clean.

Meanwhile, make veal à la king.

[3] Diet 3—substitute Rice Ring*.

Veal à la King

½ cup butter or margarine
½ cup flour[4]
¾ teaspoon salt (adjust to
taste)
¼ cup canned, French-style
green beans, cut in small
pieces

2 cups clear chicken broth[5]
2 tablespoons dry white
sherry wine
2 cups cubed cooked veal
(1-inch cubes)
2 egg yolks, slightly beaten
½ cup milk

Melt butter in medium-sized saucepan and remove from heat. Stir in flour, salt, and green beans and then gradually stir in broth, mixing well. Return to stove and, over medium heat, bring to boil, stirring constantly. Reduce heat, add wine, and simmer for 1 minute. Add veal, mixing well and bring back to boiling.

Remove from heat. Combine egg yolks with milk and stir into hot veal mixture. Cook over medium heat, stirring constantly, for about 5 minutes, or until heated through.

Remove from heat, cover, and keep hot.

To unmold noodle ring, carefully run a small spatula around edge of mold to loosen. Invert over serving platter; shake gently to release. Remove any noodles that may adhere to bottom of mold and replace on ring.

Fill center of ring with some of veal à la king and keep rest warm until ready to use.

Makes 8 servings.

Note: Turkey or chicken could be used in place of veal and, of course, a Rice Ring* could also be substituted for Diet 2, depending on preference.

[4] Diet 3—use 2 tablespoons cornstarch.
[5] If using canned chicken soup, Monarch and Richelieu brands have only salt added.

Diet: 2

VEAL CHOPS AND PARISIAN NOODLES

3 cups uncooked medium or
  broad noodles
1 can (3 or 4 ounces)
  undrained sliced
  mushrooms, finely chopped
½ cup milk
2 tablespoons flour

2 chicken bouillon cubes
2 tablespoons chopped canned
  green beans
4 loin or rib veal chops, cut
  ¾ inch thick
¼ to ½ teaspoon salt

Cook noodles in boiling salted water in a kettle, according to label directions, and drain. Return to kettle.

While noodles cook, drain liquid from mushrooms into a 2-cup measure; stir in milk and enough water to make 1½ cups.

In a small saucepan, stir liquid into flour until smooth, then stir in bouillon cubes. Cook, stirring constantly and crushing cubes, until sauce thickens and boils 1 minute. Stir in chopped mushrooms and green beans.

Pour mixture over noodles and keep hot.

Sprinkle chops lightly with salt and place on rack in broiler pan.

Broil 4 to 6 inches from heat, 8 minutes on each side, or until meat is tender.

When chops are done, place on noodles on serving plate.

Makes 4 servings.

Note: Once again, green beans are being used as a substitute for parsley. They provide the color and the texture that are so often missing from the patient's meals.

Diet: 1–2–3

BACON OR BEEF FRY

Preheat oven to 400° F.

Place rack over a cake pan and lay desired number of slices of bacon or beef fry next to each other on rack. Do not overlap slices. Place in preheated oven for about 12 minutes. Do not turn.

Dry on paper towels.

POULTRY

and Dressings

I think, and hope you will too, that the chicken recipes are tasty enough for any company meal.

Chicken, as you may know, is very perishable. If you can't buy it the day you are planning to use it, then freeze it. . . . Don't let it sit in the refrigerator, uncooked, for several days. If you have any leftovers, let your guests wait a few minutes for dessert while you refrigerate any food that you can use again. This is extremely important. Too many hostesses are so intent on rushing from one course to the other that they neglect to take proper precautions with food that will be eaten at a later date. To be a good cook means more than combining the right ingredients; you must treat food properly and do everything to avoid spoilage, which in this day and age really is quite simple if we condition ourselves to good food care habits.

Maybe I'm conceited but I think Chicken Livers in Sauce is a dish that's elegant enough to serve in your best chafing dish and not have one guest ask why you're serving diet food to everyone. If diets did not have to be considered, it would be hard to think of a spice to add that would enhance its flavor. After all, really good cooking, should never be so heavily spiced that you can't tell if you're eating beef or veal. . . . It should be well flavored, which I think these recipes are.

Diet: 1–2

BAKED CHICKEN

2 *eggs*	1 *chicken (3 pounds), cut up*
4 *tablespoons dry white or*	1 *cup flour (approximately)*
dry sherry wine	½ *cup melted butter or*
1½ *teaspoons salt*	*margarine*

Preheat oven to 350° F.

Beat eggs. Add wine and salt and mix well.

Marinate chicken parts in egg and wine mixture for 1 to 2 hours, in the refrigerator.

Dredge in flour.

Place pieces next to each other in greased baking dish and brush generously with melted butter or margarine.

Bake uncovered for about 1 hour. Turn drumsticks after about a half hour. Other pieces should be baked skin side up and do not need turning.

Makes 3 to 4 servings.

Diet: 1–2

GOLDEN CHICKEN AMERICAN

1 egg, slightly beaten
¼ cup milk
1 chicken (3 pounds), cut
  up

¾ cup crushed cheese Ritz
  crackers
⅓ cup butter

Preheat oven to 400° F.

Combine egg and milk. Dip chicken pieces in egg mixture, then dip into cracker crumbs.

Melt butter in a shallow baking pan in oven. Remove baking pan from oven. As pieces of cracker-coated chicken are placed in pan, turn to coat with butter, then bake skin side down in a single layer.

Bake for 25 minutes. Turn chicken. Bake another 25 minutes.

Makes 4 servings.

Diet: 1–2

SIMPLE BAKED CHICKEN

1 package (about 6 ounces)
  cheese crackers, crushed
  fine
2 teaspoons salt

½ cup salad oil
2 broiler-fryers (about 3
  pounds each), cut in
  serving-size pieces

Preheat oven to 375° F.

Place cracker crumbs in a pie plate and stir in salt. Pour salad oil into a second pie plate.

Dip chicken pieces in salad oil and then into crumbs to coat well. Place in a single layer in an ungreased large shallow pan.

Bake in moderate oven for 1 hour, or until tender and golden brown.

May be served warm or cold.

Makes 6 servings.

Diet: 1–2

SPECIAL OVEN-FRIED CHICKEN

1 fryer (3 pounds), disjointed	1 teaspoon Ac'cent
2 whole eggs	½ teaspoon salt
2 tablespoons white wine or sherry	1 stick (¼ pound) butter or margarine
	1 cup flour (approximately)

Wash and clean chicken. Do not dry. Place in a large bowl. Mix eggs, wine, Ac'cent, and salt together and pour over chicken in bowl. Marinate at least 8 hours in the refrigerator.

Preheat oven to 400° F.

Melt butter in baking dish in preheated oven. Flour chicken and place skin side down in pan. Bake for 20 minutes and turn. Bake additional 40 minutes. If chicken seems to be getting too brown, reduce heat to 350° F. Remove from pan immediately when done and chicken will not be greasy.

Can be served hot or cold.

Makes 3 to 4 servings.

Suggestion: Add small canned white potatoes to the pan during the last 15 minutes, turning once to brown.

Diet: 1–2–3[1]

CHICKEN FRICASSEE

Chicken

*About 1½ pounds chicken
legs and thighs*
*About 1½ pounds chicken
breasts*

6 cups water
*1 or 2 large carrots, scraped
and cut in 1-inch pieces*
1 teaspoon salt

Sauce

⅓ cup butter or margarine
*½ cup unsifted all-purpose
flour*[1]
1 teaspoon salt
3 cups chicken broth
¾ cup light cream

*¼ cup dry sherry or
vermouth*
*1 jar (2½ ounces)
mushrooms, drained and
chopped very fine*

Place chicken parts, 6 cups water, carrots, and salt in a 6-quart kettle and bring to boiling. Reduce heat and simmer, covered, until chicken is tender. This should take about 1 hour. Remove chicken from broth and let cool.

Cut chicken into large pieces and discard bones and skin. This will yield about 4 cups chicken.

Strain chicken broth and reserve 3 cups for sauce.

To make sauce: Melt butter in a 3-quart saucepan and remove from heat. Add flour and salt, stirring until smooth. Gradually stir in reserved broth and the cream and bring to a boil, stirring constantly. Reduce heat and add sherry or vermouth, stirring to blend. Add chicken and mushrooms to sauce and simmer, covered, 10 minutes, stirring occasionally. Makes 6 servings.

[1] Diet 3—use ¼ cup cornstarch.

Suggestion: To make this look a little more like the real thing, stir some very finely chopped canned green beans into the sauce . . . with a little imagination, this can serve as a substitute for parsley.

The chicken fricassee can be served over baked refrigerator biscuits, noodles, or rice. (Diet 3 must be limited to rice.) If using biscuits, for each serving, spoon chicken and sauce over 2 biscuit halves.

Diet: 2–3[2]

CHICKEN LIVERS IN RICH BROWN SAUCE

> 2 *chicken bouillon cubes*
> 2 *cups water*
> ½ *pound fresh chicken livers*
> 1½ *cups Rich Brown Sauce*

Place chicken bouillon cubes and about 2 cups water in a saucepan and bring to boil. Drop cleaned chicken livers into boiling broth and simmer for about 10 minutes, or until they are tender.

Add chicken livers to brown sauce. Simmer about 10 minutes, stirring frequently.

Serve over rice.

Serves 2.

Rich Brown Sauce

> 1 *teaspoon cornstarch*
>   *(optional)*
> ¼ *cup tomato juice (optional)*
> 2 *beef bouillon cubes*
> 1 *teaspoon Sanka instant*
>   *coffee*
> 1 *cup hot water*

> 2 *tablespoons butter*
> 2 *tablespoons flour[2]*
> 2 *tablespoons burgundy wine*
> ½ *jar (2½-ounce size)*
>   *mushrooms, drained and*
>   *very finely chopped*
>   *(optional)*

Put 1 teaspoon cornstarch in a saucepan, stir in the tomato juice until smooth. Bring to boil, stirring constantly until thick. Set aside and let cool.

Dissolve bouillon cubes and instant coffee in the cup of hot water and set aside.

Melt butter in saucepan and remove from heat. Stir in flour and gradually add ¾ cup of the beef broth and the tomato juice-cornstarch mixture (or add the whole cup of broth if not using the homemade tomato mixture). Return to medium heat and stir constantly until it thickens. Add wine and mushrooms and simmer about 10 minutes, stirring frequently.

Yield: 1½ cups.

² Diet 3—use 1 tablespoon cornstarch.

Diet: 1–2–3

ROAST TURKEY

METHOD I

Preheat oven to 350° F.

Wash turkey in cold running water and dry well with paper towels. Stuff and truss and place in a covered roasting pan.

Brush with ¼ pound butter or margarine. Roast, covered, 20 to 25 minutes per pound, until about 1 hour before done; then uncover and turn a few times until golden brown and crisp.

METHOD II

Preheat oven to 325° F.

Prepare turkey, as in Method I, but place in roasting pan without cover and insert meat thermometer in center of inside thigh muscle. Turkey must be roasted until internal temperature is 190° F. as this is temperature required to make certain all harmful bacteria have been killed.

If thermometer is not available, doneness may be tested by cutting between thigh and body; if juice runs clear, not pink, the bird is done.

Diet: 1–2

STUFFING

2 pounds sliced bread,
  toasted, preferably bakery
  egg bread
4 eggs, slightly beaten
¼ pound butter or margarine,
  melted
1 teaspoon salt, adjust to
  taste
The following ingredients are
  optional, any one, or all
  three, may be added for
  flavor if in accordance
  with individual diet:

1 large carrot, grated
2 large apples, peeled and
  grated
1 jar (4 ounces) mushrooms,
  very finely chopped

Place bread in large colander. Run cold water over bread for a
few minutes and then squeeze as dry as possible. Transfer to large
bowl and toss lightly with all other ingredients.

This makes enough stuffing for a large turkey up to 20 pounds.
If the turkey is small, place extra stuffing in a casserole and bake,
covered, for about 45 minutes at same temperature as turkey.

Diet: 1–2

APPLE STUFFING FOR POULTRY

8 large tart apples
½ cup cold water
2 cups pulled toasted egg
  bread

1½ tablespoons sugar
2 tablespoons melted butter
1 egg

Pare, quarter, and core the apples. Place them in a saucepan. Add the cold water, cover, and cook until the apples are tender but not broken. Cool.

Add the pulled bread, sugar, melted butter, and egg. Toss the stuffing thoroughly but gently.

Diet: 1–2

STUFFING FOR CHICKEN
OR BREAST OF VEAL

Basic Recipe

8 slices egg bread	*1 egg, beaten*
Milk	*½ teaspoon salt*
1 tablespoon butter	

Place bread in bowl and cover with milk. Soak about 5 minutes and squeeze liquid out of bread.

In a saucepan, melt butter and add broken pieces of bread, stirring until all butter is absorbed.

Cool and then add the beaten egg and salt. Mix well.

The basic recipe is sufficient for a chicken weighing 4 to 4½ pounds. Adjust according to size of fowl. This stuffing may also be used for breast of veal.

🐚 FISH

In this chapter, in addition to main course fish dishes, you will find several sandwich recipes, which I hope you will find as valuable as we did.

The diet patient, particularly if he is on a high dosage of steroids, frequently requires a snack between meals and providing a variety of sandwiches can be extremely challenging.

If the patient is a child and you're planning, for example, a birthday party where quite often hot dogs would be served, instead of making something different for the patient, why not serve everyone the Bunsteads? They can be put together in advance and have the added advantage of being served right in the foil.

Diet: 1–2–3

BAKED FISH IN WHITE WINE

1½ cups very thinly sliced
  carrots
Boiling water
1½ cups finely chopped
  canned string beans
1 can (3 ounces)
  mushrooms, drained and
  finely chopped

2 teaspoons salt
1 slice halibut (2 pounds)
3 bacon slices, cooked and
  chopped
¾ cup dry white wine[1]

Preheat oven to 375° F.

In small saucepan, cover carrots with boiling water; bring to boiling. Boil, covered, for 5 minutes. Drain.

Arrange carrots, beans, and mushrooms in bottom of large, shallow bake-and-serve pan. Sprinkle with 1 teaspoon salt.

Place fish on vegetables and sprinkle with rest of salt. Sprinkle with bacon. Pour on wine.

Cover top of pan completely with foil and bake 20 minutes.

Remove foil and bake 15 to 20 minutes longer, or until fish can be easily flaked with fork.

Serve right from pan.

Makes 6 servings.

[1] Diets 2 and 3 may use chicken broth instead of wine if they prefer.

Diet: 1–2

BAKED RICE AND FISH BALLS

2 cups flaked cooked fish
2 cups boiled rice
2 eggs, beaten
1 teaspoon salt
2 or 3 teaspoons Homemade
   Barbecue Sauce* for
   flavor (optional)

Heavy cream or evaporated
   milk
Crushed Rice Krispies or
   Wheaties

Preheat oven to 350° F.

Combine flaked fish, boiled rice, eggs, salt, and barbecue sauce and form mixture into 2-inch balls. Roll them in the cream, or evaporated milk, and then the cereal crumbs. Place them in a well-greased pan and bake for about 20 minutes.

Makes 12 two-inch balls.

Serve with homemade tomato sauce.

Homemade Tomato Sauce

1 cup tomato juice
1 tablespoon cornstarch

Combine tomato juice and cornstarch, heating mixture in saucepan, stirring until smooth, and simmering for several minutes.

Makes 1 cup.

Diet: 1–2–3[2]

FILLET OF SOLE POTATO PIE

Instant mashed potatoes for
4 servings
1 pound fillet of sole
Milk or dry white wine to
cover
2 tablespoons butter
2 tablespoons all-purpose
flour[2]

1 cup milk
½ teaspoon salt
1 can (8½ ounces) small
peas, drained
¼ cup shredded American
cheese

Preheat oven to 425° F.

Prepare instant mashed potatoes as package directs for 4 servings. Using a 1½-quart shallow casserole, which has been greased, make border of mashed potatoes.

Cut sole in 4 pieces; place in skillet and cover with milk or dry white wine. Cook over very low heat, basting frequently with the hot liquid, until sole is tender but retains shape. Lift carefully from liquid and place in potato-bordered casserole. Save ½ cup liquid.

Melt butter in saucepan. Remove from heat and gradually stir in flour. Slowly add milk and ½ cup liquid from poaching sole and cook over low flame until thickened and smooth. Add salt and adjust quantity to taste.

Stir in drained canned peas and pour over sole. Sprinkle shredded cheese over potatoes. Bake about 15 minutes or until potatoes are slightly browned.

Makes 4 servings.

[2] Diet 3—use 1 tablespoon cornstarch.

Diet: 1–2

FISH ROLL

1 pound boiled codfish or   1 teaspoon salt
   haddock   Browned bread crumbs
2 eggs, well beaten   Melted butter
2 cups mashed potatoes

Preheat oven to 375° F.

Remove all skin and bones from cooked fish and break the fish into flakes.

Mix the beaten eggs with the potatoes and salt and mix the flaked fish into the potatoes.

Shape into a roll and sprinkle with bread crumbs and melted butter.

Place in a well-buttered pan and bake for 30 minutes.

Serve with Hard-boiled Egg Sauce* or cheese sauce (see White Cream Sauce Variations).

Serves 4.

Diet: 1–2

HOT SALMON SANDWICHES

1 can (7¾ ounces) salmon,   Pinch salt
   drained, boned, and flaked   4 slices white toast
3 hard-cooked eggs, chopped   4 slices American cheese
3 tablespoons Hellman's   (or Muenster or Swiss if
   brand mayonnaise[3]   allowed on diet)

Preheat broiler.

Combine salmon with eggs, mayonnaise, and salt in top of a large double boiler. Stir over hot not boiling water until well heated. Heap mixture onto toast slices and top each with a slice of cheese; place under broiler until cheese is melted and lightly browned.

Serves 4.

[3] This amount of mayonnaise is allowed as it does not yield a highly concentrated fat mixture. Hellman's brand is recommended as it is a bland mayonnaise.

Diet: 1–2

SALMON PATTIES

1 can (7¾ ounces) salmon,
    drained
1 egg, slightly beaten

⅛ cup bread crumbs
¼ to ½ teaspoon salt
Melted butter or margarine

Bone salmon and remove all skin. Mash with fork and add egg and bread crumbs and salt. Mix well. Form into 4 patties and refrigerate at least for a half hour.

Preheat oven to 325° F.

Place in greased, shallow, oven-proof dish and brush lightly with melted butter or margarine.

Bake for about 20 minutes.

Serves 2.

Suggestion: Pour over the patties a white sauce (see White Sauce *), slightly thicker than basic recipe, to which you add a can (8½ ounces) of peas, drained, and 1 slice of American cheese for each cup of white sauce.

Diet: 1–2

SALMON TIMBALES

1 can (1 pound) salmon
⅔ cup milk (approximately)
1 or 2 teaspoons lemon juice
   (optional)
2 tablespoons butter or
   margarine
2 tablespoons flour

1 cup toasted pulled egg
   bread
½ cup finely chopped canned
   green beans
1 egg, slightly beaten
Hard-boiled Egg Sauce*

Preheat oven to 350° F.

Drain the salmon, reserving the liquid and adding enough milk to make 1 cup liquid.

Remove the bones and skin from the salmon and flake with a fork. Sprinkle with lemon juice.

Melt butter in a saucepan over low heat, add flour and mix well. Gradually add the milk mixture and stir constantly over low heat until thickened. Add salmon, bread, green beans, and egg and stir lightly.

Spoon into greased custard cups, place in a pan of hot water, and bake for about 30 minutes.

After baking, turn out of the custard cups and serve with Hard-boiled Egg Sauce*.

Serves 4.

Diet: 1–2–3[4]

TUNA SANDWICH

1 can (7 ounces) tuna (packed in oil)
2 hard-cooked eggs

Do not drain off oil. Lift the tuna out of the can and leave oil in can. In a bowl, mash the tuna and the hard-cooked eggs together and add some of the oil to moisten the mixture thoroughly. Depending on personal preference, all of the oil may be added. Spread on toast.

Makes 3 to 4 sandwiches.

[4] Diet 3 will, of course, only be able to use this on type of bread or crackers allowed on Gluten-free Diet.

Diet: 1–2

BUNSTEADS

¼ pound American cheese, cut into ½-inch cubes

1 can (7 ounces) tuna, drained and flaked

3 hard-cooked eggs, finely chopped

6 tablespoons finely chopped canned green beans

4 ounces whipped cream cheese

1 tablespoon sour cream

½ to 1 teaspoon salt

10 frankfurter rolls, split

Preheat oven to 325° F.

In medium bowl, combine all ingredients, except rolls, and mix well.

Spoon mixture into rolls. Wrap each roll in foil; place on cookie sheet and bake 25 minutes.

Serve hot, right in foil. It would be advisable to remove them from the oven about 5 or so minutes before you're ready to serve them to avoid burned fingers and tongues, as they do become quite hot.

Serves 10.

Note: Depending on number of portions desired, either cut recipe in half or make entire quantity and refrigerate unused portion. Do not spread tuna mixture on rolls until ready to bake.

 EGGS

Egg Dishes, Pancakes, and Omelets

With many of these dishes, as with others throughout the book, the person preparing the food may find that the non-skillet method of preparation is not only the healthier way and equally as tasty, but in most instances, really quite simple. Scrambled eggs, for instance, prepared the conventional way, require almost your constant attention, whereas the double boiler method leaves you freer to prepare the other items that will be served with the eggs. And, just so no one feels sorry for the patient who is deprived of his skillet-prepared scrambled eggs, I would like to point out that the double boiler method is the gourmet way.

The baked French Toast, though it takes longer to prepare in the oven, loses none of the flavor and allows you to make the entire quantity at one time. The skillet method makes it very difficult for everyone to eat at the same time, particularly the person in charge of cooking.

Some cooks are frightened by lengthy recipes, such as the German Pancake with Apple Filling. Please don't be.

Though elegant when served, it's really quite simple. Some recipes look simple because they are brief but when you start working with the recipes you realize that their brevity is due to the fact that they are not very explicit. Brevity has been sacrificed here as I feel the less taken for granted about the cook's previous knowledge and experience, the simpler the recipe will be.

Diet: 1–2–3

UN-FRIED "FRIED" EGG

Grease a small casserole that can be placed in pot containing boiling water.

Drop egg into casserole and cook, uncovered, until white is desired firmness.

Diet: 1–2–3

SCRAMBLED EGG A LA GOURMET

3 eggs	*⅛ teaspoon salt*
3 tablespoons half and half	*1 tablespoon butter*

Beat eggs and add half and half and salt. Combine well.

Grease upper part of double boiler and melt butter over hot water. Add egg mixture. When mixture begins to thicken, shred with fork. For creamier eggs, stir with wooden spoon.

Makes 2 servings.

Note: For variety, cube half of a 3 ounce package of cream cheese and stir into eggs after they start to thicken slightly. Continue cooking until eggs thicken and cheese melts.

Diet: 1–2

BAKED EGGBURGERS

4 hamburger buns, unsliced   4 eggs
3 tablespoons melted butter   ¼ teaspoon salt
2 tablespoons grated   Butter
  Parmesan cheese (or
  American, if Parmesan not
  allowed)

Preheat oven to 325° F.

Remove centers of buns to make shells. Put centers in oven until toasted, then crumble. Brush shells inside and out with melted butter. Sprinkle each with cheese and break an egg in each. Season with salt and top with toasted crumbs. Dot with butter and bake for 15 to 20 minutes.

Serves 4.

Diet: 1–2–3[1]

EGGS AU GRATIN

3 to 4 hard-boiled eggs   ¼ cup (approximately)
¼ cup butter or margarine   grated cheese of type
¼ cup flour   allowed
1 teaspoon salt
2 cups milk
4 tablespoons grated
  American cheese (or
  Parmesan, if allowed)

Preheat broiler.

Slice the eggs into a buttered pie pan and cover with rich cheese sauce, made as follows:

Melt butter in saucepan and remove from heat. Gradually blend in flour and salt and mix well. Slowly stir in milk. Cook over medium heat, stirring constantly until thick and smooth. Remove from heat and stir in 4 tablespoons grated cheese until melted.

After cheese sauce has been poured over eggs, sprinkle the top surface with finely grated (¼ cup) cheese and place under broiler until hot and bubbly.

¹ Diet 3 must, of course, use double white sauce recipe made with cornstarch, to which you add 4 tablespoons grated American cheese.

Diet: 1–2–3

FAKE EGG FOO YONG

3 measuring cup ounces rice   ⅛ teaspoon salt
3 eggs   1 tablespoon butter
3 tablespoons half and half
  or milk

Cook rice as directed on package. Keep covered and set aside.

Beat eggs and add half and half and salt. Grease upper half of double boiler and melt the butter over hot water. Add egg mixture and stir from time to time, preferably with wooden spoon. When eggs are still slightly loose, gradually stir in rice and mix well.

Serve hot.

Makes 2 servings.

Note: This is also very good if you let the egg and rice mixture get quite firm and pour brown sauce over it. See Rich Brown Sauce*.

Diet: 1–2

FRENCH TOAST

1 tablespoon butter   *2 tablespoons milk*
1 egg, slightly beaten   *2 slices white bread*

Preheat oven to 375° F.

Melt butter in shallow baking dish in oven. Beat egg and milk together. Dip bread in egg and milk mixture and soak until liquid is absorbed.

Place soaked bread slices next to each other in dish with melted butter and bake until light brown. Turn until other side is light brown. Do not overbake. Total baking time, approximately 20 to 25 minutes.

Basic recipe serves 1.

Note: For variety, substitute juice, as allowed on diet, for milk and serve warmed fruit on toast.

Diet: 1–2–3

BAKED OMELET

6 eggs, separated   *⅓ cup water*
1 teaspoon salt   *2 cups sauce of your choice*
¼ cup cornstarch

Preheat oven to 350° F.

Grease two 9-inch pie plates. Use pottery or heat-proof glass, not metal. Heat 5 minutes in oven.

Beat egg whites with 1 teaspoon salt to soft peaks. Beat egg yolks thick and lemon-colored, then beat in cornstarch and water. Fold into the beaten whites.

Divide mixture equally into hot pie plates. Bake for 15 minutes or until set. Immediately turn out onto serving dish, one omelet on top of the other and with sauce poured between and over top.

Makes 4 to 6 servings.

Suggestions for sauces: cheese sauce (see White Cream Sauce Variations *), Fruit Sauce *.

Diet: 1–2

EGG AND BACON OMELET

12 slices day-old bread,   4 eggs
  preferably egg bread   2½ cups milk
½ to ¾ pound grated   ¼ teaspoon salt
  American cheese
6 to 8 slices bacon, baked
  or broiled crisp and
  chopped

Trim crusts from the bread and lay 6 slices in the bottom of buttered 12×7×2-inch baking pan. Cover the bread with half the cheese and half the bacon. Lay remaining bread on and repeat. Beat eggs well with milk and salt and pour over the bread slices. Let stand at least 30 minutes in refrigerator. Preheat oven to 325° F. Bake for 40 to 50 minutes.

Makes 6 servings.

Note: This is an excellent late evening snack as it may be put together and refrigerated for several hours before baking.

Diet: 1–2

GERMAN PANCAKE WITH APPLE FILLING

Apple Filling

¼ cup butter
1 pound apples, peeled, cored, and thinly sliced
¼ cup granulated sugar

Melt butter in medium-sized saucepan. Stir apples into melted butter; continue stirring, over medium heat, for several minutes. Gradually add sugar and stir well. Allow mixture to cook for about 7 or 8
minutes, stirring often. If apples are not tender at this point, though
they should not be too soft, cover pan and steam for about 5 minutes. Cool to lukewarm before using. Filling may be made several
hours in advance, refrigerated, and then reheated before pouring
onto pancake.

Peaches may be substituted for apples and prepared in same
manner. Canned peaches may be used by heating them in their own
juice without the butter and sugar.

Batter

3 large eggs (¾ cupful)
¾ cup cool milk
½ teaspoon salt
¾ cup sifted all-purpose flour
1 tablespoon butter

4 tablespoons melted butter
*2 tablespoons granulated
sugar*
*2 tablespoons confectioners'
sugar*

Preheat oven to 450° F.

Combine eggs, milk, salt, and flour in a medium-sized bowl. Beat
about 2 or 3 minutes with electric beater or eggbeater. Melt the
tablespoon butter in a 10- or 11-inch heavy aluminum or cast-iron
skillet. (If skillet of this type is not available, two glass or pottery
pie plates may be substituted and batter and butter divided between
them.) When very hot, pour batter into it and bake about 15 min-

utes. Lower heat to 350° F. and bake about 10 minutes more, or, until golden brown and crisp.

When pancake puffs up in center during baking, puncture well with a fork. When done, turn out on a long platter. Drizzle about 2 tablespoons butter and 2 tablespoons granulated sugar over entire surface. Spread half the pancake with warm apples and fold it over to enclose apples.

Drizzle top with remaining hot melted butter and the 2 tablespoons confectioners' sugar. Cut crosswise and serve at once.

Serves 2 as main course or 4 to 6 as dessert.

Diet: 1–2

PETITE PANCAKES

2 cups sifted flour	*2 cups milk*
4 teaspoons baking powder	*1 tablespoon melted butter*
1 teaspoon salt	*or margarine*
2 eggs, separated	*Honey Butter*

Preheat oven to 350° F.

Sift dry ingredients together. Beat egg yolks; stir in milk and melted butter or margarine; beat into dry ingredients until smooth. Beat egg whites until they form soft peaks; fold into batter mixture.

Grease cookie sheet and drop a scant tablespoon of batter for each cake onto it, leaving several inches between cakes. Bake for 2 or 3 minutes; turn and bake until underside is golden. Keep warm until all are baked. Stack 8 pancakes high on heated plates and serve with honey butter.

Makes 8 servings, 8 cakes each.

Note: Batter may be made ahead, then covered and chilled. Stir well before baking.

Honey Butter

Melt 1 cup (2 sticks) butter or margarine in a saucepan; stir in 1 cup honey; heat 1 to 2 minutes longer.

Makes 2 cups.

ॐ CHEESE

Some of the recipes in this chapter, such as Cheese Soufflé and Macaroni and Cheese, may be considered either as main courses or side dishes. This will depend on the patient. Some people feel they must have meat, fowl, or fish with every meal or it is not a meal, while others prefer to skip these items on occasion.

If one of these dishes is to be the main course, you could consider serving with it a hot vegetable, canned green beans with the Mock Vinegar and Oil Salad Dressing*, or a mold, and if you precede it with soup and also have a dessert, it is a more than adequate meal.

Diet: 1–2

MELTED AMERICAN CHEESE SANDWICH

2 tablespoons butter or margarine
2 slices bread (preferably egg bread)
2 slices American cheese

Preheat broiler to 400° F.

Cut butter in little pieces and divide evenly between the 2 pieces of bread. Place bread, with butter, on cookie sheet lined with aluminum foil or on foil broiler pan and place under broiler for about half a minute to a minute, just long enough for butter to have melted sufficiently to make spreading easier.

After butter has been spread, place 1 piece of bread buttered side down. On this, place 2 slices American cheese and cover with other slice of bread, buttered side up (dry side touching cheese).

Return to broiler and turn once as bread starts to brown slightly and brown other side slightly.

Serves 1.

Diet: 1–2

HOT CHEESE SUPPER SANDWICH

2 tablespoons flour or 1   *2 cups cooked or canned*
* tablespoon cornstarch*   * green beans*
8 ounces tomato juice (make   *Butter*
* certain that brand used has*   *4 slices bread*
* only salt added)*   *4 slices American cheese*

To make sauce, blend together, in a saucepan, flour or cornstarch and tomato juice. Boil 5 minutes, stirring constantly. Add green beans. Stir occasionally.

Preheat broiler.

To make the cheese sandwich, spread butter on one side of each bread slice. Top each with slice of cheese. Place on baking sheet and broil 2 minutes, or until cheese is melted. Top with sauce and serve at once.

Serves 2.

Diet: 1–2–3[1]

CHEESE SOUFFLE

4 tablespoons butter	½ pound sliced American
4 tablespoons flour[1]	cheese
1 teaspoon salt	6 eggs, separated
1½ cups milk	

Melt butter in top of double boiler. Add flour, salt, and milk to make white sauce, stirring constantly. Melt cheese in white sauce, continuing to stir. When melted, cool slightly.

Preheat oven to 300° F.

Beat egg yolks and add slowly to cooled cheese mixture. Beat whites until stiff and fold into sauce until white disappears.

Pour into *un*greased casserole (about 3- to 4-quart capacity) and bake for 1 hour and 10 to 15 minutes.

Makes 4 servings.

[1] Diet 3—use 2 tablespoons cornstarch.

Diet: 1–2

CHEESE SOUFFLE WITH TURKEY OR CHICKEN

12 slices well-buttered egg
  bread, including crusts, cut
  into cubes
1 pound American cheese,
  grated
4 whole chicken breasts,
  cooked and cut up or 4
  cups cut-up white meat of
  turkey

2½ cups milk
4 eggs
2 teaspoons salt

Butter a large (3-quart) casserole well. First put in a layer of bread
(½ of the bread cubes), sprinkle with one-third of the grated cheese,
and cover with half of the cut-up chicken or turkey. Repeat these
three layers and sprinkle with the remaining cheese. Combine milk,
eggs, and salt in a mixing bowl and beat well. Pour egg and milk
mixture over ingredients in casserole. Refrigerate overnight.

Bake in preheated 350° F. oven for 1 hour.

Serves 6 to 8.

Diet: 1–2

MACARONI AND CHEESE—METHOD 1

2 cups (8 ounces) elbow
  macaroni
3 tablespoons butter
3 tablespoons flour
½ teaspoon salt

1 cup heavy cream
½ cup dry white wine
2 cups (about 8 ounces)
  grated American cheese

Cook macaroni according to package directions. Drain and reserve. Preheat oven to 350° F.

Melt butter. Remove from heat. Stir in flour and salt. Slowly add the cream and wine and cook over low heat, stirring constantly until thickened. Add the cheese and stir until melted. Mix together the macaroni and cheese sauce and put into a greased 1½-quart casserole.

Bake for 15 minutes or until thoroughly heated through.

Serves 4 to 6.

Diet: 1–2

BAKED MACARONI AND CHEESE— METHOD 2

1 package (8 ounces) elbow macaroni

2 cups (about ½ pound) grated American cheese

¼ cup butter or margarine

¼ cup unsifted all-purpose flour

2 cups milk

1 teaspoon salt

Preheat oven to 375° F.

Cook macaroni as label on package directs and drain.

In a 1½-quart shallow baking dish, alternate macaroni (in two layers) with 1½ cups cheese (in two layers) and set aside.

To prepare sauce, melt butter in medium-sized saucepan and remove from heat. Blend in flour, gradually stir in milk, then salt. Bring to boiling, stirring constantly. Boil 1 minute.

Pour sauce over macaroni and cheese in casserole. Top with remaining cheese.

Bake 15 to 20 minutes, or until cheese is melted and browned slightly.

Makes 4 to 6 servings.

Diet: 1–2

MACARONI AND CHEESE LOAF

½ cup macaroni
½ cup milk
2 eggs, beaten
2 tablespoons melted butter

½ cup soft bread crumbs
¾ cup grated American
cheese
¼ teaspoon salt

Preheat oven to 325° F.
Cook macaroni according to package directions. Scald milk, stir in beaten eggs and melted butter; pour mixture over macaroni. Add remaining ingredients and mix well. Put into a buttered loaf pan and bake for 50 minutes.
Serves 2.

Diet: 1–2

MACARONI RING

1 package (8 ounces)
macaroni
2 cups hot milk
¼ pound butter

2 cups (½ pound) shredded
American cheese
2 teaspoons salt
2 eggs, beaten

Cook macaroni as instructed on package and drain.
Preheat oven to 350° F.
Combine macaroni with other ingredients and toss lightly to blend.
Turn into a well buttered 10-inch ring mold. Set in pan of hot water and bake for 35 minutes, or until set.
Unmold on warm platter and fill center with cubed cooked meat; or as desired.
Makes 6 to 8 servings.

Diet: 1–2

MACARONI CHEESE SALAD

*1 package (8 ounces) elbow
  macaroni*
⅔ cup hot water
*6 ounces American cheese,
  diced*
1 tablespoon cream cheese

½ teaspoon cornstarch
2 hard-cooked eggs, chopped
*1 can (8½ ounces) small
  peas, drained*
½ teaspoon salt

Cook macaroni as directed on package. Drain and rinse with cold water.

Add hot water to diced American cheese and cream cheese in a small saucepan. Heat over medium heat, stirring constantly until cheeses are melted.

In a small dish, make smooth paste of cornstarch and about 3 tablespoons of the cheese sauce. When smooth, add to sauce in pan and continue to stir until smooth and slightly thickened. Cool.

Blend macaroni, eggs, peas, and salt. Fold in cheese sauce.

Chill several hours before serving.

Makes 6 servings.

Diet: 1–2

COTTAGE CHEESE PUFF

Egg and Milk Mixture

1 cup cottage cheese
3 eggs
½ cup milk

2 tablespoons melted butter
¼ teaspoon salt

Salmon (tuna or chicken) Mixture

1 cup flaked salmon (tuna   *¼ teaspoon salt*
*   or chicken)*   *12 slices bread, crusts*
1 cup cottage cheese   *   removed*
½ cup finely chopped canned
*   green beans*

Preheat oven to 250° F.

Put 1 cup cottage cheese, eggs, milk, butter, and salt in blender
and blend until almost smooth. If no blender is available, first beat
cottage cheese with an electric mixer until almost smooth; add other
ingredients and beat well.

Combine salmon (or tuna or chicken), 1 cup cottage cheese,
chopped green beans, and salt.

Put half the bread in the bottom of 6 individual casseroles; spoon
salmon mixture over the bread and top with remaining bread. Pour
egg and milk mixture over all. Let casseroles stand in refrigerator
at least 1 hour.

Bake for 45 minutes or until mixture is set.

Makes 6 servings.

🌱 VEGETABLES

Unfortunately, many people are not vegetable lovers. . . . We, who do love them, have tried to analyze this and feel very strongly that the method of preparation employed when we were children had a great deal to do with our present attitude.

I recall an incident that happened to a young lady who not only disliked carrots, she HATED them. She was invited for dinner by friends who did not know of this dislike and, as luck would have it, the hostess prepared carrots with a delicious sweet-sour sauce that, unfortunately, cannot be incorporated in a diet cookbook. The young lady, being well mannered, took the minimum portion possible on her plate and forced herself to eat it out of politeness, as she gathered it was one of her hostess's prized recipes. It was when she voluntarily took a second, and much larger helping, that she confessed her previous dislike for carrots . . . but she also admitted she had never had them served in any way except canned and heated in their own liquid.

The non-carrot loving patient should be sport enough to try Carrot Cheese Pie and Carrot Ring at least once.

I can't guarantee that he will suddenly become a carrot lover, though it's a possibility, but I can guarantee that neither dish tastes like canned carrots that have just been heated and served.

At a dinner party, the Carrot Ring, filled with peas, looks so much more festive than merely filling a serving bowl with a can of peas . . . it's almost as if there were a sign on the dish that said, "In case someone likes vegetables."

Any vegetable, when combined with other ingredients, takes on an entirely new flavor.

After preparing the Baked "French Fried" Potatoes, I wonder if you'll go back to the deep-fried method if you're preparing "fries" for someone who is not on a diet?

It is sincerely hoped that you will also feel that all of these potato dishes are appetizing enough for company and not just a special side dish to be prepared for the patient.

I have, for example, served Potato Soufflé at numerous dinner parties and received compliments each time. Even when not confronted with diet problems, many hostesses take the path of least resistance when it comes to potatoes and either bake, roast, or mash them. The Potato Soufflé really takes just a little more effort than mashing potatoes.

Diet: 1–2–3

CREAMED GREEN BEANS

1 can (1 pound 1 ounce) French-style green beans
1 carton (4 ounces) whipped cream cheese
2 tablespoons half and half

Heat and drain canned green beans. To the drained beans add the cream cheese and half and half. Heat gently, stirring until sauce is creamy, and serve.
Serves 4.

Diet: 1–2–3

HONEY BEETS

1 can (1-pound size) whole   *¼ cup honey*
  beets (not pickled), drained   *½ teaspoon salt*
¼ cup butter or margarine

Preheat oven to 350° F.
Place beets in a baking dish, dot with butter, and pour honey over all the beets. Season with salt. Cover and bake for about 1 hour, basting occasionally.
Serves 4.

Diet: 1–2

CARROT CHEESE PIE

Buttered bread slices   *½ cup grated carrots*
  (approximately 5), crusts   *2 eggs*
  trimmed off (Egg bread is   *1 cup milk*
  tastier than plain white)
4 ounces grated American
  cheese

Preheat oven to 350° F.
Generously butter a 9- or 10-inch Pyrex pie pan. Line the pan with the slices of bread, buttered side down, cutting to fit the bottom and sides.
Put grated cheese and carrots on top of bread.
Beat the eggs with milk and pour over the cheese mixture.
Bake for 30 minutes.
Serves 4.

Note: This may be put together several hours ahead and refrigerated until about 30 minutes before placing in oven.

Diet: 1–2

CARROT RING

¾ cup Crisco or Spry
¼ cup brown sugar
1 egg
1 cup grated carrots
1 teaspoon baking powder

1¼ cups flour
½ teaspoon baking soda
1 tablespoon hot water
2 to 3 tablespoons bread
    crumbs

Preheat oven to 350° F.

Mix as you would a cake—stir shortening until smooth, gradually add sugar, making sure there are no lumps, add egg, and blend ingredients well. Add carrots and mix well. Stir baking powder into flour and dissolve soda in hot water. Gradually stir in flour, alternating with a little of the hot water and soda mixture.

Grease a 6-cup size ring mold well and sprinkle with bread crumbs. "Dish" mixture into mold and then put mold into pan of water. Bake 1 hour.

Unmold. May be filled with peas or other vegetables.

Serves 6 to 8.

Note: If you have any left over, wrap it in foil and place in 350° F. oven for about 30 minutes to reheat.

Diet: 1–2

LETTUCE SOUFFLE

1 cup boiling water
1 teaspoon salt
1 cup shredded head lettuce

2 slices dry bread
3 eggs, separated

Preheat oven to 350° F.

Bring water and salt to boil and add lettuce. Cover pan and cook over very low heat for 3 to 5 minutes. Drain and cool. Roll dry bread into crumbs. Beat egg yolks until light yellow and mix with crumbs and lettuce. Beat whites until stiff and fold into lettuce mixture. Put in baking dish and bake for 10 minutes.

Serves 2 to 3.

Note: The above recipe is acceptable only if the individual's specific diet permits cooked spinach.

Diet: 1–2–3[1]

SPINACH SUPERB

2 packages (10 ounces each)   ¼ cup sugar
   frozen chopped spinach   1 teaspoon salt
⅛ pound butter or margarine   1 cup liquid from spinach
¼ cup flour,[1] sifted

Cook spinach according to package directions. Reserve 1 cup liquid from cooked spinach. In a saucepan, brown butter until quite dark. Blend together flour, sugar, salt, and liquid from spinach. Heat this mixture together with spinach and browned butter for approximately 5 minutes. *Watch closely,* as it will burn easily.

Serves 4.

[1] Diet 3—use 2 tablespoons cornstarch.

Diet: 2–3

RICE AND SPINACH PILAF

1 can (13¾ ounces)   3 cups packaged precooked
   chicken broth²   rice
2 chicken bouillon cubes   1¼ cups chopped, cooked
3 tablespoons butter or   spinach
   margarine   1 teaspoon salt
1¼ cups water

In medium saucepan, combine chicken broth with bouillon cubes, butter, and 1¼ cups water. Bring to boiling. Add rice. Cover and remove from heat. Let stand 5 minutes.

Fluff up rice with fork. Add spinach and salt and toss lightly to combine. If using canned spinach, be sure to heat it first.

Makes 10 servings.

Note: If spinach is not allowed, or desired, substitute sliced carrots or experiment with other vegetables, as allowed on diet.

² Monarch and Richelieu brands have only salt added.

Diet: 1–2

SPINACH NOODLE RING

1 package (8 ounces)   ¼ pound butter
   broad noodles   1 pound chopped cooked
½ cup half and half or milk   spinach
3 eggs   1 teaspoon salt

Cook noodles as label on package indicates.

Preheat oven to 350° F.

Combine cooked noodles with all other ingredients and pour into well-greased ring mold. Place ring mold in pan containing 1 inch of water and bake for 1 hour.

Serves 6 to 8.

Diet: 1–2–3

SPINACH AND POTATO CASSEROLE

3 eggs, beaten
½ cup butter, melted
1 teaspoon salt
1 cup grated Parmesan or
Swiss cheese (as allowed)
1 pound (about 8 medium-
sized) potatoes, peeled and
shredded

2 (10-ounce) packages
frozen chopped spinach,
thawed and drained

Preheat oven to 350° F.

Combine the eggs, two-thirds of the butter, the salt, and ½ cup of the grated cheese. Pour the mixture over the potatoes and blend well. Put ½ of the potato mixture into a greased 2-quart casserole. Top with the spinach and cover with the remaining potato mixture. Sprinkle with the remaining ½ cup of cheese and the remaining butter. Bake for 1¼ hours, or until the potatoes are cooked. The top of the casserole should have a golden crust.

Serves 4 to 6.

Note: This goes well with roast chicken or duck.

Diet: 1–2

VEGETABLE AU GRATIN

1¾ cups chopped spinach or   6 baked patty shells
    carrots   2 tablespoons shredded
1 cup White Sauce*   cheese

Preheat oven to 350° F.
Combine spinach, or carrots, with cup of white sauce.
Fill the baked patty shells. Crumble the caps from patty shells
and mix with the shredded cheese (of type allowed on diet). Sprinkle
over the filling and bake for 15 minutes.
Serve hot.
Serves 6.

Diet: 1–2–3

DUCHESS POTATOES

4 medium-sized potatoes,   2 tablespoons butter or
    cleaned, pared, and cut up   margarine
1 egg yolk   1 teaspoon salt

Cook potatoes in lightly salted boiling water in a medium-sized
saucepan for 20 minutes, or until tender; drain well, then shake pan
gently over low heat to dry and fluff potatoes; remove from heat.
Break up potatoes with a masher, then beat in egg yolk and
butter or margarine until fluffy and smooth. Season with teaspoon
salt, taste, and adjust to personal preference.
May be spooned in fluffs around meat and baked until tipped
with gold.
Makes 8 servings.

Diet: 1–2–3

BAKED "FRENCH FRIED" POTATOES

1 large Idaho potato
¼ to ½ cup salad oil

Preheat oven to 375° F.

Peel potato and cut as for french fries. Place potatoes in large bowl and pour oil over them. Turn potatoes to make certain they are all well coated. Remove potatoes from oil and spread flat, next to each other, in cake pan, or on cookie sheet, lined with aluminum foil. *DO NOT* use oil left over in bowl.

Bake for about 30 to 40 minutes or until potatoes are lightly browned and tender. Turn them at least once during this time.

Remove from pan and place on thick pad of paper towels; blot thoroughly on all sides.

Serves 1 to 2.

Diet: 1–2

MASHED POTATO BALLS

6 medium-sized potatoes   *Melted butter—approximately*
3 tablespoons butter   *4 tablespoons*
1 teaspoon salt   *Rice Krispies crumbs*
1 egg, beaten

Preheat oven to 375° F.

Clean, pare, and quarter potatoes. Cook potatoes in boiling water until done, about 30 minutes. Drain well, mash, and add the

3 tablespoons butter and 1 teaspoon salt. Beat with fork until creamy. Add beaten egg.

Roll potatoes into balls. Roll balls in melted butter and then Rice Krispies crumbs. Place in greased pan and bake until well heated.

Makes 4 servings.

Note: These can be made in advance and reheated when ready to serve.

Diet: 1–2–3

POTATO CHEESE PUFFS

2 eggs, separated
1⅓ cups mashed potatoes,
*   hot or cold*
3 tablespoons hot milk
⅓ cup grated American
*   cheese (or other type if*
*   allowed)*

¼ to ½ teaspoon salt
1 tablespoon very finely
*   chopped canned green*
*   beans (optional)[3]*
1½ tablespoons soft butter

Preheat oven to 350° F.

Beat the egg yolks. Add the mashed potatoes, hot milk, and grated cheese, and beat until fluffy. Season with salt and add green beans.

Beat egg whites until stiff and fold into potato mixture. Place batter in 6 mounds in a greased pan and dot tops with the soft butter.

Bake for 20 minutes.

Makes 6 puffs.

[3] The green beans are suggested as they add color, texture, and flavor.

Diet: 1–2–3

POTATO PUREE

5 medium-sized potatoes   1 teaspoon salt
3 tablespoons butter   1 cup milk, scalded

Peel, quarter, and wash the potatoes; put potatoes in cold water and boil until tender, about 30 minutes.

Preheat oven to 325° F. Heat oven-proof dish.

Drain potatoes, mash with fork, and then beat with electric mixer, adding butter, salt, and scalded milk gradually.

Beat until light and fluffy. Pile onto hot oven-proof dish and reheat in the oven for a few minutes.

Serves 6.

Diet: 1–2–3

POTATO SOUFFLE

5 medium-sized potatoes   1 cup milk, scalded
3 tablespoons butter   3 eggs, separated
1 teaspoon salt

Peel, quarter, and wash the potatoes; put potatoes in cold water and boil until tender, about 30 minutes. Drain, mash with fork, and then beat with electric mixer, adding butter, salt, and scalded milk gradually. Beat until light and fluffy. Cool slightly.

Preheat oven to 350° F. Heat baking dish.

Add 3 well-beaten egg yolks and mix well.

Fold in the stiffly beaten egg whites and turn into hot buttered baking dish.

Bake about 30 minutes.

Serves 6.

Note: You can have this recipe all ready, up to the point of adding the egg whites, before your company arrives. Half an hour or so before you're ready to serve, you need only heat the buttered dish and while that is heating, beat the egg whites to snow, fold into the purée to which you had previously added the egg yolks, place in the oven, and forget about it for 30 minutes.

Diet: 2–3

ROAST POTATOES

¼ cup butter or margarine	*½ tablespoon salt*
4 large baking potatoes	*¼ cup chicken broth[4]*

Preheat oven to 350° F.

Melt butter in a baking dish large enough to hold the potatoes side by side.

Pare potatoes and roll them in the melted butter, coating them well. Sprinkle with salt.

Bake, uncovered, 1 hour. Remove pan from oven and turn potatoes. Pour chicken broth over potatoes and bake about 30 minutes more, turning several times.

Makes 4 servings.

[4] If using canned broth, Monarch and Richelieu brands have only salt added.

Diet: 1–2–3

CANDIED SWEET POTATOES

4 sweet potatoes　　　　　*2 tablespoons butter*
½ cup brown sugar　　　　*½ cup sherry wine*

Scrub and boil the potatoes until tender, 20 to 30 minutes.
Preheat oven to 350° F.
Peel and cut in slices.
Put into a buttered baking dish in layers, with a little brown sugar over each layer. Dot each layer with butter and add a little sherry.
Bake for ½ hour.
Serves 4.

Diet: 1–2–3

FANCY SWEET POTATOES

4 large sweet potatoes　　　*1 tablespoon Madeira wine*
1 tablespoon cream　　　　*1 small banana, mashed*
2 tablespoons butter　　　　*Sour cream, if allowed on*
1 teaspoon salt　　　　　　　*diet*

Preheat oven to 450° F.
Bake potatoes for 1 hour, or until done. Cut a slice from top of each potato and scoop out insides. Add cream, butter, and salt to the potatoes.
Beat until light and fluffy. Stir in wine and mashed banana and return to oven in baking dish for about 5 minutes at 350° F.
If allowed sour cream, garnish potatoes with it.
Makes 4 servings.

Note: Can be attractively served in scooped-out orange shells.

Diet: 1–2–3

SWEET POTATO CASSEROLE

8 cups (about 8 pounds)   2 teaspoons salt
   mashed sweet potatoes   2 cups miniature
⅛ pound butter   marshmallows
½ cup brown sugar

Preheat oven to 350° F.
Cook potatoes until tender.
Peel and mash. Add butter, brown sugar, and salt. Place in a large
buttered casserole dish (or two small ones) and sprinkle marsh-
mallows on top.
Bake for about 30 minutes or until marshmallows melt and start
to sink in.
Makes 10 to 12 one-cup servings.

Diet: 1–2–3

BAKED YAMS AND APPLES

3 small yams or sweet   6 tablespoons butter
   potatoes (1 pound)   ½ cup light brown sugar
3 large apples (1 pound)   ¼ cup cold water

Wash yams or sweet potatoes and boil with skins on until just
barely tender, about 20 minutes. Drain and cool.
Preheat oven to 475° F.
Wash, peel, core, and cut the apples into eighths.
Butter a 10-inch oven-proof glass pie plate with 2 tablespoons
butter.

Peel sweet potatoes and cut into pieces, approximately the same size as the apples.

Arrange apples and sweet potatoes attractively in dish, dot with 4 tablespoons butter and sprinkle with light brown sugar and cold water.

Bake until apples are tender and beginning to brown . . . about 40 minutes. Baste once or twice as they cook.

Serve hot.

Serves 4.

 # RICE
and Other Side Dishes

Eating potatoes with every meat course can become monotonous, even to the non-diet person.

Rice is, of course, an excellent substitute. Though we generally tend to think of serving rice only if the main course dish has lots of gravy, I feel Rice au Gratin, as it does not have the usual dry consistency of rice, is an excellent accompaniment to gravyless meat or fowl dishes or, for that matter, fish.

If you're looking for something really different in the way of a side dish, all I can say is try Gnocchi with Tomato.

Diet: 1–2–3

RICE AU GRATIN

½ cup rice   *6 slices (1 ounce each)*
1 cup water   *American cheese*
¼ teaspoon salt

Put rice, water, and salt in medium-sized saucepan and bring to full boil. Turn heat down low and cover with tight lid and simmer.

After about 5 to 7 minutes, when half of the water has been absorbed by rice, cut American cheese into small pieces and stir into rice. Cover again and continue to simmer for about 7 to 10 minutes more, until balance of water has been absorbed. Rice will, of course, be moister than usual, due to cheese sauce, but this makes a tasty side dish, expecially when main dish has no gravy.

Keep covered until ready to serve.

Makes 3 to 4 servings.

Diet: 2–3

RICE WITH CHICKEN BROTH AND EGGS

3 cups chicken broth[1]   *3 eggs*
1 cup rice   *¼ cup melted butter*
1 teaspoon salt

Bring the chicken broth to a boil in the top of a double boiler. Slowly stir in the rice and salt and cook, tightly covered, over hot water, until rice is tender. This will take at least 30 minutes. Stir it frequently.

Beat the eggs with the melted butter and stir mixture into rice. Makes 2 servings.

[1] If using canned broth, Monarch and Richelieu brands have only salt added.

Diet: 1–2–3

RICE RING

2 cups uncooked rice	½ cup grated American
2 teaspoons salt	cheese
4 cups cold water	2 tablespoons butter

Put rice in pot with salt and cold water and bring to boil fast over high heat. Cover and turn heat low for 14 minutes, or until water has evaporated.

Stir in grated cheese and butter.

Pack in greased mold, bringing rice well up to top of mold. Put mold in pan of hot water, cover with waxed paper until ready to unmold and serve.

Makes 6 to 8 servings.

Diet: 1–2

GNOCCHI WITH TOMATO

2½ cups milk
1 cup cream of wheat
3 tablespoons butter or
    margarine
1 egg yolk

¼ teaspoon salt
8 ounces tomato juice
1 tablespoon cornstarch
½ cup grated American
    cheese

Lightly grease a 10×6×1½-inch baking dish.

In medium saucepan, heat milk just until film forms on surface, but do not boil.

Over low heat, sprinkle in cream of wheat; cook, stirring, until mixture is thickened and heavy . . . about 5 minutes.

Remove from heat. With wooden spoon, beat in 1 tablespoon butter, egg yolk, and salt until mixture is smooth and well combined.

Spread evenly in prepared dish.

Refrigerate until firm, about 2 to 3 hours.

When refrigeration time is almost up, preheat oven to 425° F.

Slowly stir tomato juice into cornstarch and heat. Blend well so there are no lumps.

With sharp knife, cut gnocchi into 2-inch squares. Arrange, overlapping, in 9-inch pie plate. Dot with remaining butter; spoon tomato mixture over top; sprinkle with cheese.

Bake 10 or 15 minutes or until bubbly.

Makes 4 servings.

Diet: 1–2

FARINA DUMPLINGS

⅓ cup sifted all-purpose
   flour
1 teaspoon baking powder
½ teaspoon salt
⅔ cup farina

1 egg, beaten
¼ cup milk
1 tablespoon butter or
   margarine, melted

Sift flour with baking powder and salt into medium-sized bowl. Add farina, mixing well.

Combine egg with milk and butter. Add to flour mixture, stirring until smooth.

In a 3-quart saucepan, bring 6 cups lightly salted water to boiling.

Drop farina mixture, by slightly rounded teaspoonfuls, into boiling water.

Cover tightly, reduce heat, simmer 15 minutes.

Drain dumplings well and serve hot with stew or other type dish that has gravy.

Makes 20 dumplings.

Diet: 1–2–3

BANANA IN BACON BLANKET

Preheat oven to 350° F.

Peel and cut into quarters, crosswise, desired number of firm ripe bananas. Sprinkle them very lightly with sugar and roll each piece in a very thin slice of bacon. Secure bacon with toothpick and bake the bananas until the bacon is crisp.

 # SAUCES

and Salad Dressings

This chapter heading will, most likely, puzzle the reader, who probably thinks it's impossible to create a salad dressing that adheres to the diet and still tastes like salad dressing, and, as salads, per se, are taboo, what's the point in bothering?

Though I had a great feeling of accomplishment each time I was able to serve my guinea pig patient a new dish, nothing compared with the reward of first the questioning look and then the smile of appreciation when my new dish was a mock version of something terribly taboo in its usual form and perfectly acceptable as prepared. This applied in particular to Homemade Barbecue Sauce, Mock Vinegar and Oil Salad Dressing, and Homemade Catsup.

The Homemade Barbecue Sauce, which was created specifically for the Barbecued *Beef* Spareribs, through experimentation became a staple condiment. It is surprisingly versatile and can add an interesting new flavor to a cream cheese sandwich or be the "spice" of a casserole.

Even though the patient cannot have lettuce, he may actually crave the taste of the dressing more than the lettuce itself. Why not find out by serving cold canned green beans with the Mock Vinegar and Oil Salad Dressing? It may just soothe that craving.

For anyone who can't eat hamburgers without catsup, it should not be difficult to imagine the reception the hamburgers received the night they were served with Homemade Catsup after the patient had been subjected to eating them plain for several years.

For some reason, many quite experienced cooks adopt an attitude about white sauces that frightens the average cook from even trying because they feel only an expert can accomplish this culinary feat. These "experienced" cooks really aren't as experienced as all that or they would not find it so difficult, or perhaps their trick is to keep you from trying it so you won't discover how simple that delightful sauce of theirs was to put together.

I feel the biggest trick here, as with so many recipes, is to be realistic about the amount of cooking time you will need for the meal you are preparing. If a sauce wll take about 5 minutes of your time, you can't speed it through in 2 nor can you let it cook by itself for 5 minutes while you're rushing around doing other things, that is unless you happen to like lumpy white sauce.

Most people have forgotten how to make white sauce because a great many recipes don't even call for it; they suggest instead that you use any one of a number of creamed canned soups.

This is not to say that your casserole made with a homemade white sauce will be superior to the same casserole made with canned soup. After all, the soup people have been in business for years. All I'm trying to say is, if you want your patient to be in business for years, carefully read the list of ingredients on these canned soups and decide if it's really worth taking a chance serving him something that contains so much onion and spice or whether it wouldn't be a better idea somehow to juggle your time so you come out with an extra 5 or so minutes and can prepare your own sauce.

In my opinion the whole key to a successful, smooth sauce lies in reading the instructions and following them. When the butter has melted, *remove* the saucepan *from heat. Gradually* stir in flour (or cornstarch) means just that . . . gradually. If you add it quickly, you can't control it and you'll have a mess of lumps that are harder to get rid of than they are to avoid in the first place. Again, the recipe says *slowly* stir in milk and, though speed is a relative thing, I hardly think you should interpret slowly as meaning pour it all in at once. The key words are in italics . . . *remove from heat, gradually,* and *slowly.* If you concentrate on these words, you will control the sauce and put all those experienced cooks in their place by telling them you can't understand why they find sauce-making such a feat when you find it so simple.

Diet: 1–2–3

WHITE SAUCE MADE WITH CORNSTARCH

2 tablespoons butter or	*½ teaspoon salt*
margarine	*1 cup milk*
1 tablespoon cornstarch	

Melt butter in saucepan; blend in cornstarch and salt. Remove from heat and slowly stir in milk. Cook over medium heat, stirring constantly, until sauce thickens. Then boil 1 minute.

Yield: 1 cup.

Note: For thicker sauce, use 3 tablespoons butter and 2 tablespoons cornstarch for each cup milk.

Diet: 1–2

WHITE SAUCE MADE WITH FLOUR

¼ cup butter or margarine	*1 teaspoon salt*
¼ cup flour	*2 cups milk*

Melt butter in saucepan and remove from heat. Gradually blend in flour and salt and mix well. Slowly stir in milk. Cook over medium heat, stirring constantly until thick and smooth.

Yield: 2 cups.

WHITE CREAM SAUCE VARIATIONS

Based on 1-cup recipe

Diet: 1–2

2 tablespoons butter	½ teaspoon salt
2 tablespoons flour	1 cup milk

Diet: 1–2–3

2 tablespoons butter	½ teaspoon salt
1 tablespoon cornstarch	1 cup milk

Diet: 2–3

Substitute chicken broth[1] for milk.

Diet: 2–3

Substitute fish broth for milk.

Diet: 1–2–3

Beat 1 egg, add half of the white sauce to the egg slowly and add this combination to the rest of the sauce.

Diet: 1–2–3

Add 1 chopped hard-boiled egg.

Diet: 1–2–3

Add 2 tablespoons grated American cheese and stir until melted.

Diet: 1–2–3

Add 2 tablespoons dry white wine or sherry and let sauce come to a boil.

[1] If using canned broth, Monarch and Richelieu brands have only salt added.

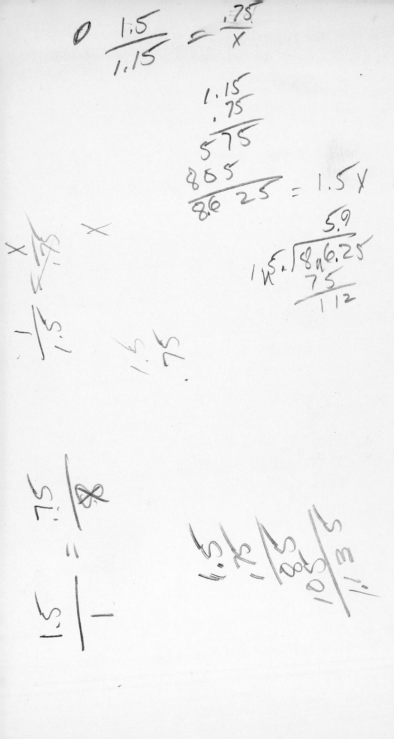

0   $\dfrac{1.5}{1.15} = \dfrac{.75}{x}$

$$\begin{array}{r} 1.15 \\ \times\ .75 \\ \hline 575 \\ 805 \\ \hline 8.6\ 25 \end{array} = 1.5\,x$$

$$\begin{array}{r} 5.9 \\ 1.5.\overline{)8.6.25} \\ 75 \\ \hline 1\,12 \end{array}$$

$\dfrac{x}{1.5}$ x

$\dfrac{1}{1.5}$

$\dfrac{75}{8}$ = $\dfrac{1.5}{1}$

$\dfrac{1.5}{75}$

Diet: 1–2–3

HOMEMADE BARBECUE SAUCE

2 teaspoons Sanka instant
  coffee
½ cup boiling water
½ cup tomato juice

2 teaspoons cornstarch
½ teaspoon salt
2 tablespoons burgundy wine
¼ cup sugar

Combine all ingredients, dissolving coffee in hot water and gradually stirring tomato juice into cornstarch before adding to other ingredients. Simmer for 10 minutes, stirring occasionally. Let cool slightly, pour into jar with tight lid, and refrigerate.

Yield: 1 cup.

Note: In addition to using this sauce for beef spareribs, it can be used as a flavoring agent in a variety of things. Try it on meat loaf or even a cream cheese sandwich and neither will be bland.

Diet: 1–2–3[2]

MUSHROOM WHITE SAUCE

3 tablespoons butter
3 tablespoons flour[2]
1½ cups milk
¾ teaspoon salt

½ jar (2½-ounce size)
  mushrooms, drained and
  finely chopped

Melt butter in saucepan. Remove from heat and gradually stir in flour, then milk and salt. Cook over medium heat, stirring constantly until sauce thickens. Add mushrooms.

[2] Diet 3—use 1½ tablespoons cornstarch.

Diet: 1–2–3[3]

HARD-BOILED EGG SAUCE

2 hard-boiled eggs
4 tablespoons butter
4 tablespoons all-purpose
    flour[3]

2 cups hot milk
½ teaspoon salt

Hard boil the eggs.

Melt the butter in the top of a double boiler over direct low heat. Stir in the flour and cook for a minute or two, stirring constantly with a wooden spoon. Gradually add the hot milk, making a smooth cream sauce. Season lightly with about ½ teaspoon salt.

Keep hot over hot water.

Remove the shells from the eggs and slice them into the sauce.

Yield: 2 cups.

Note: Good with boiled salmon or any boiled fish.

[3] Diet 3—substitute 2 tablespoons cornstarch.

Diet: 2

MUSHROOM SAUCE

1 beef bouillon cube
6 ounces boiling water
1 tablespoon flour

1 or 2 tablespoons very
    finely chopped canned
    mushrooms

Dissolve bouillon cube in hot water. Gradually stir broth into flour and continue stirring until smooth. Add mushrooms and heat.

Yield: ½ cup.

Diet: 2–3[4]

RICH BROWN SAUCE

1 teaspoon cornstarch
    (optional)
¼ cup tomato juice
    (optional)
2 beef bouillon cubes
1 teaspoon Sanka instant
    coffee
1 cup hot water

2 tablespoons butter
2 tablespoons flour[4]
2 tablespoons burgundy wine
½ jar (2½-ounce size)
    mushrooms, drained and
    very finely chopped
    (optional)

Put 1 teaspoon cornstarch in a saucepan, stir in the tomato juice until smooth. Bring to boil, stirring constantly until thick. Set aside and let cool.

Dissolve bouillon cubes and instant coffee in the cup of hot water and set aside.

Melt butter in saucepan and remove from heat. Stir in flour and gradually add ¾ cup of the beef broth and the tomato juice-cornstarch mixture (or add the whole cup of broth if not using the homemade tomato mixture). Return to medium heat and stir constantly until it thickens. Add wine and mushrooms and simmer about 10 minutes, stirring frequently.

Yield: 1½ cups.

[4] Diet 3—use 1 tablespoon cornstarch.

Note: Though this sauce was created to go with chicken livers, (see Chicken Livers in Rich Brown Sauce) it is far more versatile. It can, for example, be used over leftover slices of beef and served with mashed potatoes.

For the oriental touch, you could make the scrambled eggs and rice recipe, Fake Egg Foo Yong, letting the eggs get quite firm, and pouring the sauce over. For a little more of the Egg Foo Yong texture, add some chopped canned green beans to the eggs and rice. With a little imagination, many basic recipes, such as this one, can be adapted to meals the patient was fond of prior to being put on the diet.

Diet: 1–2–3

HOMEMADE TOMATO SAUCE

1 cup tomato juice
1 tablespoon cornstarch

Combine tomato juice and cornstarch, heating mixture in saucepan, stirring until smooth, and simmering for several minutes.
Makes 1 cup.

Diet: 2–3[5]

SAUCE FOR FISH

2 tablespoons butter   *⅓ cup light or heavy cream*
2 tablespoons flour[5]   *¼ teaspoon salt*
1 cup fish or vegetable   *2 egg yolks*
* stock*   *2 tablespoons dry white wine*

Melt butter and remove from heat. Stir in flour and gradually add stock. Cook over medium heat, stirring constantly until sauce is smooth and starts to boil. Reduce heat and stir in cream and salt. Remove from heat.

Beat the egg yolks slightly. Place pan with sauce over hot water or transfer to top of a double boiler and add the egg yolks and wine. Stir until it has thickened slightly.

Yield: about 1⅓ cups.

[5] Diet 3—use 1 tablespoon cornstarch.

Diet: 1–2–3[6]

SPAGHETTI SAUCE

½ to ¾ pound ground beef   *2 tablespoons burgundy wine*
2 cups tomato juice   *2 tablespoons brown sugar*
2 tablespoons cornstarch   *½ teaspoon salt*

Preheat broiler.

Place meat in oven-proof casserole, preferably one that may also be placed on stove. Place meat under broiler and periodically break meat up with fork and turn so it browns evenly.

In a measuring cup, or bowl, gradually stir tomato juice into the cornstarch until mixture is smooth.

When meat is lightly browned, remove from broiler. Stir in the tomato juice-cornstarch mixture and place over medium heat on stove. Add wine, sugar, and salt and continue to stir until mixture starts to thicken and comes to a boil. Reduce heat and simmer covered for about 10 minutes, stirring occasionally.

Adjust flavor to suit personal taste by increasing wine, sugar, or salt. When adding wine, always allow sauce to boil a few more minutes as it is in the boiling process that the alcohol evaporates, making the use of wine permissible.

Serves 2.

[6] Diet 3—though spaghetti is not allowed on the Gluten-free Diet, the above sauce contains no objectionable ingredients and may be used on rice dishes.

Diet: 1–2–3

HOMEMADE CATSUP

1 teaspoon cornstarch   *¼ teaspoon salt*
½ cup tomato juice   *1 teaspoon sugar*
1 tablespoon burgundy wine

Place cornstarch in saucepan and gradually stir in tomato juice, making smooth paste. Add other ingredients, stirring until mixture comes to a boil. Simmer for 10 minutes and remove from heat. When slightly cooled, place in jar with tight cap and refrigerate. Yield: ½ cup.

Note: Attention must be called to the fact that some brands add more than just salt to the tomato juice. Always read labels and take nothing for granted.

As no preservatives are added to this catsup, it is advisable to make it in small quantities as it cannot be kept as long as the commercially bottled kind.

Diet: 1–2–3

HOMEMADE MAYONNAISE

1 egg yolk   *1 cup salad oil*
1 teaspoon sugar   *1 tablespoon vinegar*
½ to 1 teaspoon salt

Beat yolk at medium speed, in electric mixer, for 4 minutes. Add sugar and salt and then add half of the oil, drop by drop. When mixture begins to thicken, gradually add vinegar and then add rest of oil more freely, beating constantly at medium speed. Time required: about 20 minutes.

Yield: 1 cup.

Diet: 1–2–3

MOCK VINEGAR AND OIL SALAD DRESSING

5 tablespoons burgundy wine   *4 tablespoons oil*
¼ teaspoon sugar   *¼ teaspoon salt*

Place 5 tablespoons wine and ¼ teaspoon sugar in a saucepan and boil rapidly for a few minutes, stirring several times. Cool mixture. When cool, combine with oil and salt and mix very thoroughly. Adjust to taste by adding more salt, wine mixture, or oil.

Serves 2.

Note: Serve as salad dressing over canned, drained vegetables, such as string beans, beets, or asparagus (if allowed).

ॐ CASSEROLES

The introduction recognized the fact that if your patient is male, there is a good possibility he may not like (or he thinks he may not like) casseroles. I trust that by the time you reach this chapter either the patient, you, or preferably both of you, has the courage to give a few casseroles a try. If they are acceptable to the patient, think of how greatly enhanced his variety of meals will be.

Though the circumstances in each patient's home are different as to the activities of the housewife and the size of the family, generally speaking, today's housewife does not confine her time to cleaning house and slaving over a hot stove 7 days a week. If she works, her cooking time on weekdays is particularly limited. You just can't put a roast in the oven at 6 o'clock, unless you're used to eating quite late in the evening.

The casserole is a double boon to her and she would be wise

to plan it for her busiest days rather than one of those stay-at-home days when she has time to make a roast.

One advantage to the casserole is that it does not, generally, necessitate several side dishes. Most of the casseroles contain meat, fish, or fowl, a vegetable, and a starch. All that is really required with it is a mold or a canned vegetable salad with either Home-made Mayonnaise or Mock Vinegar and Oil Salad Dressing.

The second advantage is the ease with which it can be prepared at dinner time. Yes, it does take longer to put together than it takes to remove a steak from the refrigerator and place in the broiler but there's no law that says it must be put together just prior to placing it in the oven.

If you're going to be gone from home most of the day until about 45 minutes before you must have dinner on the table, prepare your casserole in the morning, or the evening before. Instead of baking it, refrigerate it until you actually want it baked. If you think about it, this is really easier than rushing home, trying to figure out if the potatoes will get done by dinner time, watching the steak, and preparing a vegetable. If the cook is herself the patient, she should welcome the casserole as it should leave her far more relaxed at mealtime if she hasn't had all that hustle and bustle just prior to eating.

Diet: 1–2–3

BEEF-RICE CASSEROLE

1½ cups uncooked rice
1½ pounds ground beef
1½ teaspoons salt
¼ to ½ cup Homemade
   Catsup*

1 can (1 pound) green
   beans, drained
1½ cups Mushroom White
   Sauce*

Preheat broiler.
Cook rice according to package directions and drain. Spread in

greased, shallow 1½-quart baking dish. Cook meat under broiler until it loses its red color, breaking up with fork. Spread meat on rice. Set oven at 350° F. Sprinkle meat with salt and spread with catsup. Cover with beans. Top with Mushroom White Sauce and even top with spoon. Bake for about 40 minutes.

Makes 6 servings.

Diet: 1–2

MOCK LASAGNE

1 pound ground beef
2 cups tomato juice[1]
2 tablespoons cornstarch
4 cups water
1 tablespoon salt
8 ounces broad noodles

1 teaspoon salt
1 cup cottage cheese
8 ounces cream cheese
½ cup chopped canned
*   French-style green beans*
¼ cup dairy sour cream

Preheat broiler.

Place meat in shallow oven-proof dish and place under broiler. Check frequently and break meat up with fork. Keep breaking up meat and turning it until it has lost its red color. Drain off fat.

Gradually add tomato juice to cornstarch, in a bowl, and stir until smooth. Add tomato juice mixture to meat and heat this in a saucepan, or the oven-proof dish, if it can also be used on direct heat.

Bring 4 cups water and 1 tablespoon salt to a boil in a large saucepan. Add noodles and bring to full boil. Boil 2 minutes, stirring frequently. Cover and let stand 10 minutes. Drain and rinse in hot water.

Preheat oven to 350° F.

Put half of the noodles in bottom of shallow baking dish. Mix 1 teaspoon salt, cheeses, string beans, and sour cream. Spread

this mixture on noodles. Add remaining noodles. Pour meat mixture over top.

Bake about 30 minutes.

Makes 6 servings.

Note: This dish can be made ahead. Put entire casserole together,
as indicated above, cover, and refrigerate until ready to bake.
Allow extra baking time so food is thoroughly heated.

[1] Make sure the tomato juice you select has only salt added and no spices.

Diet: 1–2

NOODLE, BEEF, AND SPINACH CASSEROLE

½ *pound ground chuck*	*1 egg, slightly beaten*
½ *pound fresh, canned, or*	¼ *cup butter*
frozen spinach, cooked,	½ *cup flour*
drained, and chopped	*1 teaspoon salt*
⅔ *cup grated Parmesan*	*2 cups chicken broth*[2]
cheese (or American	*2 cups milk*
cheese) as allowed	*2 egg yolks*
⅓ *cup dry bread crumbs*	*8 ounces wide egg noodles*

Preheat broiler.

Place meat in shallow oven-proof dish and place under broiler.
Check frequently and break meat up with fork. Keep breaking
up meat and turning it until it has lost its red color. Drain off fat.

Combine spinach, meat, ⅓ cup grated cheese, crumbs, and egg.
Set aside.

Melt butter. Stir in flour and salt. Gradually stir in chicken broth
and milk. Cook, stirring constantly until sauce thickens; then cook
1 minute. Blend a small amount of the hot sauce into the egg
yolks and then stir into sauce.

Cook noodles according to directions on package and drain.

Preheat oven to 375° F.

Cover the bottom of a greased 2½-quart casserole with one-
third of the sauce; add half of the noodles and half of the

spinach-meat filling. Repeat this procedure. Cover with sauce and sprinkle with remaining grated cheese.

Bake for 20 minutes or until sauce is bubbling.

Serves 4.

[2] If using canned chicken soup, Richelieu or Monarch brand have only salt added.

Diet: 1–2–3[3]

"TZIMMES"
—MEAT AND CARROT CASSEROLE

2 pounds fat brisket of beef, cut up	2 tablespoons flour[3]
½ teaspoon salt	3 large raw potatoes, pared
2 bunches carrots, cleaned	1 egg, slightly beaten
2 medium sweet potatoes, pared	½ teaspoon salt
1 tablespoon brown sugar	2 tablespoons flour[3]
	2 tablespoons fat

Salt meat and let stand. Slice carrots and sweet potatoes and place in kettle with meat. Cover with boiling water and cook 1 hour, or until meat is tender.

Measure out 1 cup of the hot carrot, potato, meat liquid and to this, gradually, add sugar and flour.

Pour back in kettle with meat, carrots, and sweet potatoes and cook slowly for 10 minutes. Pour mixture into a well-greased casserole that measures approximately 11×11×3 inches.

Preheat oven to 325° F.

Grate potatoes. Add egg, ½ teaspoon salt, 2 tablespoons flour, and softened fat to grated potatoes and mix well. Spoon grated potato mixture into ingredients in casserole and bake uncovered for 1½ hours and covered for additional ½ hour. Total baking time is about 2 hours, or until golden brown.

Serves 3 to 4.

[3] Diet 3—use 1 tablespoon cornstarch.

Diet: 1–2

EGGS AND GREEN BEANS AU GRATIN

*1 package (9 ounces) frozen
French-style green beans*
¼ cup butter or margarine
*¼ cup unsifted all-purpose
flour*
2 cups milk
1 teaspoon salt

*1 tablespoon dry sauterne
wine*
6 hard-cooked eggs, sliced
¼ cup fine bread crumbs
*½ cup grated American
cheese (or Swiss cheese if
allowed)*

Cook beans as package label directs; drain and set aside.
Preheat oven to 375° F.

Melt butter in medium-sized saucepan. Remove from heat. Blend
in flour, then milk. Add salt. Bring to boiling, stirring constantly.
Simmer for 2 minutes, adding wine while simmering.

Layer beans, eggs, and sauce in 1½-quart casserole. Combine
crumbs and cheese; sprinkle over top. Bake 20 minutes.

Serves 2 to 3.

Diet: 1–2–3

GOLDEN EGG CASSEROLE

*3 tablespoons butter or
margarine*
3 tablespoons cornstarch

½ teaspoon salt
1 cup milk
4 eggs, separated

Preheat oven to 350° F.

Melt butter and blend in cornstarch and salt. Gradually add milk and cook, stirring until smooth and thickened. Remove from heat and gradually pour over beaten egg yolks, mixing well. Beat egg whites until stiff. Spoon into greased shallow 1½-quart baking dish. Make four depressions in egg whites and spoon in sauce mixture. Set in pan of warm water and bake for 45 minutes, or until lightly browned.

Makes 4 servings.

Diet: 1–2

NOODLES AND COTTAGE CHEESE CASSEROLE

8 ounces broad egg noodles	*½ to ¾ teaspoon salt*
1 egg	*⅓ cup bread crumbs*
1 pound small curd cottage cheese	*¼ cup butter, melted*

Cook noodles according to package directions and drain. Mix slightly beaten egg into cottage cheese and add salt to taste.

Preheat oven to 375° F.

Using a greased 2-quart casserole, add layers of noodles, cottage cheese, noodles, cottage cheese and, finally, noodles.

Mix bread crumbs wth melted butter and spread on top.

Bake for 30 to 35 minutes.

Serves 6 to 8.

Diet: 1–2–3⁴

SALMON OR CHICKEN CASSEROLE

2 cups cooked white rice
(about ¾ cup uncooked
rice)
2 cups White Sauce*
2 tablespoons sauterne wine
1 jar (2½ ounces)
mushrooms, chopped very
fine, and 4 tablespoons
juice

1 can (7¾ ounces) salmon,
drained, skinned, and boned
or 2 cups diced, cooked
chicken
1 can (1 pound size)
French-style green beans,
drained

While rice is cooking, make basic white sauce. When sauce begins
to thicken, add wine, chopped mushrooms, and juice from mushrooms and continue stirring over low heat until sauce has thickened
properly. Let sauce cool slightly.

Preheat oven to 350° F.

In mixing bowl, combine all ingredients and mix well.

Turn into greased 1½-quart casserole and bake 25 to 30 minutes.
Makes 4 to 6 servings.

Note: If prepared in advance, refrigerate until ready to bake but
allow approximately 15 minutes additional time so food will be
heated thoroughly.

⁴ Diet 3—make double quantity of basic White Sauce made with Cornstarch* recipe.

Diet: 1–2

TUNA CASEROLE

8 ounces elbow macaroni
1 large can (13 ounces)
    evaporated milk
1½ cups grated American
    cheese

1 can (7 ounces) tuna,
    drained and flaked
1 teaspoon salt

Preheat oven to 325° F.

Cook macaroni according to package directions; drain and combine with evaporated milk, 1 cup grated American cheese, tuna, and salt. Toss until well blended. Put mixture into a greased 2-quart casserole and sprinkle with remaining ½ cup grated cheese.

Bake for 30 minutes.

Serves 4.

Diet: 1–2

TUNA MACARONI CASEROLE

1 package (7 ounces) elbow
    macaroni
1 can (7 ounces) tuna fish

½ cup Rice Krispies crumbs
2 teaspoons melted butter

Cook elbow macaroni according to directions on package. Drain and rinse with cold water.

Drain can of tuna fish. Separate into large flakes. Do not mince.

Make crumbs by putting Rice Krispies in a plastic bag, closing off top, and running rolling pin over bag. Stir crumbs into melted butter until they are well coated.

Preheat oven to 375° F.

White Sauce

¼ cup butter or margarine   2 slices American cheese
¼ cup flour   1 can (8½ ounces) small
1 teaspoon salt   peas, drained
2 cups milk

Melt the butter or margarine. Remove from heat. Blend in flour
and salt and mix well. Slowly stir in milk. Cook over low flame,
stirring constantly. When it begins to thicken slightly, add the American cheese (broken up into small pieces) and continue stirring until
sauce is thick and smooth. Stir in the peas.

Grease a 2-quart oven-proof casserole. Arrange a layer of elbow
macaroni, sprinkled with half of the fish, and pour one-third of the
white sauce over this. Repeat layer of elbow macaroni, remainder
of fish, and another one-third of white sauce. Cover with remaining
elbow macaroni and pour balance of white sauce over this. Cover
top with buttered Rice Krispies crumbs.

Place dish in hot oven until sauce begins to bubble, about 30 to
45 minutes.

Makes 4 large servings.

🌿 CAKES

I realize that in this jet age, the tendency is to buy rather than to bake cakes, and many bought cakes are far better than some homemade ones we've eaten. However, in dealing with the diet patient, buying cakes can be more difficult than it seems and a great deal of caution must be exercised.

It has been my experience that the sales clerks in a bakery haven't the remotest idea what ingredients are used in the various cakes they sell. In dealing with these clerks, I have stressed that the cake is to have absolutely no nuts or even almond extract in it, only to get it home and in tasting it find some of each. In some instances it may not even be the clerk's fault. That particular cake is perhaps always made without nuts but, the day it was bought, the baker must have had some nuts left over from something else and, rather than waste them, he decided to be creative and added them to that normally harmless pound cake.

The safest cakes you can buy are the frozen or other pre-packaged kind that have all the ingredients clearly listed on the label.

However, as I'm not selling cakes but inviting you to bake your own, let me merely say that none of these recipes is that complicated and the little extra effort involved is well worth the genuine appreciation usually given for homemade baked goods.

Diet: 1–2

POUND CAKE

½ pound butter
½ pound fine granulated
  sugar
5 eggs, separated

½ teaspoon vanilla
½ pound sifted cake flour
⅛ teaspoon salt

Preheat oven to 350° F.

Cream butter until very light and creamy. Add sugar a little at a time, continuing to mix until very light.

Beat egg yolks until thick and lemon-colored. Add to butter and sugar, mixing well. Add vanilla. Gradually add the sifted flour and salt and mix until smooth.

Beat egg whites until stiff but not dry and fold into the batter.

Pour into a 9×5×3-inch loaf pan which has been well buttered and lined with buttered white paper.

Bake about 1¼ hours, until golden brown and slightly shrunken from the sides of the pan. Cool before removing from pan.

Serves 8 to 10.

Diet: 1–2

BASIC TWO-EGG CAKE

Flour	½ teaspoon salt
¼ pound butter	2 teaspoons double-acting
1 cup sugar	baking powder
2 eggs, beaten	½ cup milk
1¾ cups sifted cake flour	½ teaspoon vanilla

Preheat oven to 375° F.

Thoroughly butter two 9-inch layer cake pans. Sprinkle with flour and shake each pan until it is evenly covered with a thin film of flour. Pour off any excess flour.

With a wooden spoon, cream butter well and gradually add sugar. Mix until very light and fluffy. Add beaten eggs and mix well.

Sift together flour, salt, and baking powder and add, alternately with the milk, to the butter mixture. Beat well but only enough to mix thoroughly. Add vanilla.

Divide the batter between the two pans and bake for 25 to 30 minutes.

Turn out onto a wire-mesh cake cooler and turn over immediately so the cake cools with the top of the layer up.

If using electric mixer, observe above directions and do not over-beat.

Serves 8.

Diet: 1–2

COFFEE CAKE RING

½ cup soft butter
1 cup granulated sugar
2 eggs, beaten slightly
1 cup sour cream
2 cups sifted flour

1 teaspoon baking powder
1 teaspoon baking soda
Pinch salt
1 teaspoon vanilla

Preheat oven to 350° F.
Cream butter and 1 cup sugar. Add eggs, and blend well. Stir in sour cream.
Sift together flour, baking powder, baking soda, and salt. Blend into sour cream mixture. Stir in vanilla. Pour into well-greased 10-inch ring mold.
Bake for 45 to 50 minutes.
Cool 10 minutes and remove from pan.
When completely cool, dust with confectioners' sugar.
Serves 8.

Diet: 1–2

GUGELHUPF—AUSTRIAN COFFEE CAKE

1 cup butter or margarine
2 cups sugar
6 eggs, separated
1½ cups sifted all-purpose
    flour
½ teaspoon salt

2 teaspoons baking powder
6 tablespoons milk
1 teaspoon vanilla
12-cup size gugelhupf pan
    (Turk's-head mold)[1]
Confectioners' sugar

Preheat oven to 350° F.

Cream butter to consistency of mayonnaise. Add sugar slowly while continuing to cream. Beat until light and fluffy. Beat in egg yolks, one at a time. Mix and sift flour, salt, and baking powder. Combine milk and vanilla. Add flour mixture and milk alternately to butter mixture, stirring in gently but thoroughly. Beat egg whites stiff but not dry; fold in thoroughly. Spoon into well-greased cake pan, as indicated above.

Bake for about 1 hour and 10 minutes, or until cake tests done. To test doneness, insert wooden toothpick into cake. If toothpick comes out clean, cake is done. Cool in pan 10 minutes. Loosen cake gently around rim and tube and invert on cake rack. Finish cooling. Dust with confectioners' sugar.

Serves 10 to 12.

Note: It is extremely important that the cake form is well greased. When you think you've greased it well, hold it under a light and check all the grooves, for if you've missed any, the cake will stick to the pan. The vegetable spray-on coating sold in an aerosol container works even better than greasing the form with a shortening.

[1] If you have the smaller, 6-cup size Turk's-head mold, this recipe works out extremely well using half of all the ingredients.

Diet: 1–2

BANANA CAKE

2 medium-sized bananas	*1 teaspoon baking soda*
½ cup butter	*⅛ teaspoon salt*
1 cup sugar	*½ cup milk combined with*
2 eggs	*1 heaping tablespoon sour*
2 cups sifted cake flour	*cream*
2 teaspoons baking powder	*Confectioners' sugar*

Preheat oven to 325° F.

Mash bananas and set aside.

Cream butter and sugar. Add eggs and beat approximately 5

minutes. Blend mashed bananas in well. Sift together dry ingredients and add alternately with combined milk and sour cream.

Bake in lightly greased ring mold for 45 minutes to 1 hour. Test with toothpick until toothpick is dry when removed. Cool about 10 minutes.

Just before serving, sprinkle with confectioners' sugar.

Serves 8.

Diet: 1–2

GERMAN CHEESE CAKE OR FRUIT CAKE

Dough

4 tablespoons butter (soft)	Pinch sugar
1 egg	1½ cups (approximately)
Pinch salt	sifted flour

Preheat oven to 375° F.

Stir butter until smooth. Stir whole egg with fork and add to butter. Add salt, sugar, and flour. Work ingredients with wooden spoon until ready to knead. Knead until hands are clean of dough and nothing sticks. Roll out to desired size and place on lightly greased 10-inch cake pan with spring. Bring dough up on sides and flute edge. Cut dough a few times for air to escape.

Filling

3 egg yolks	1 large (16 ounces) and 1
7 tablespoons sugar	small (8 ounces) container
2 tablespoons sour cream	small curd cottage cheese
1 tablespoon flour	3 egg whites

Add egg yolks, sugar, sour cream, and flour to cottage cheese. Beat egg whites to snow and fold into cottage cheese mixture. Pour filling over dough and bake for 1 hour. Doneness may be tested by releasing spring on cake pan and lifting cake up gently with spatula to see that dough is lightly browned.

Note: This same dough may be used with a fruit filling, such as 3 jars of drained and pitted cherries or plums, instead of cheese.

If using fruit filling, top with the following: 2 egg yolks combined with 2 tablespoons sugar. Beat 2 egg whites to snow and fold into yolk mixture until evenly distributed. Pour over fruit, after fruit has been placed on dough. Bake in preheated 375° F. oven for 45 to 50 minutes or until topping and bottom of cake dough are slightly brown. The bottom can be seen by releasing spring on the cake pan and lifting cake up gently with spatula.

Diet: 1–2

CUSTARD ZWIEBACK CAKE

½ cup sugar
⅓ cup butter, melted
1 box Zwieback, rolled into fine crumbs and sifted

Preheat oven to 300° F.
Add sugar and melted butter to sifted Zwieback and set aside.

Custard

3 egg yolks, beaten
½ cup sugar
2 cups milk
1 teaspoon vanilla
Pinch salt
1 tablespoon cornstarch
(mixed with a little cold milk)

3 egg whites
3 tablespoons confectioners' sugar

Cook above ingredients except egg whites and confectioners' sugar in top of double boiler until custard consistency. Put three-quarters of Zwieback mixture in a square pan and spread custard on it.

Beat 3 egg whites and add 3 tablespoons confectioners' sugar. Spread this on top of custard. Top with remaining Zwieback. Bake for 30 to 40 minutes. Cool in pan. Serve directly from pan.

Serves 6 to 8.

Diet: 1–2

STRUDEL DOUGH

½ *pound shortening (½*   *Seedless jam*
  butter and ½ margarine)   *1 egg white*
2 cups flour   *Confectioners' sugar*
½ pint vanilla ice cream

Cut shortening into flour with pastry cutter (or 2 forks). Add softened vanilla ice cream. Let stand overnight in refrigerator.
Preheat oven to 350° F.
Divide dough into three parts. Roll each into a thin rectangle. Fill with allowed fruit, such as apricot jam. Fold long sides in and brush each roll with egg white. Place on cookie sheet and bake for approximately 30 to 35 minutes.
While still hot, cut into 1-, 1½-, or 2-inch slices, as desired, and put in paper cupcake cups. Sprinkle with confectioners' sugar.

♣ COOKIES
and Fudge

Though there are good cookies on the market that are acceptable to the diet patient, I just don't think they are like homemade butter cookies; they're not even like homemade butter cookies that have been made with margarine.

If you store them in a metal container, such as an empty coffee can, they will stay fresh for quite some time.

In the case of the Coffee Butter Bits it would be advisable to find a shallower tin for storage than a coffee can as they are quite fragile. I must admit, however, that my experience has been that storage presents little or no problem because they disappear too quickly.

Regarding Counterfeit Chocolate, I suggest that you say nothing about it to the patient; make it, ask him to close his eyes, and give him a piece to try. Make his imagination go to work . . . this is probably the closest thing he has had to chocolate in a long while, unless he's been cheating on his diet.

Diet: 1–2

ALL PURPOSE COOKIE

½ cup cornstarch   ¾ cup margarine or butter
½ cup confectioners' sugar   ½ teaspoon vanilla (optional)
1 cup sifted flour   Confectioners' sugar
Dash salt

Preheat oven to 300° F.

Sift cornstarch, confectioners' sugar, flour, and salt together into mixing bowl. Blend in margarine (or butter) and vanilla with spoon, mixing until a soft, smooth dough forms.

Shape cookie dough into 1-inch balls. Place about 1½ inches apart on ungreased cookie sheet; flatten with lightly floured fork. (If dough is too soft to handle, cover and chill in refrigerator about 1 hour.)

Bake until edges are lightly browned, about 20 to 25 minutes. Dust with confectioners' sugar.

Makes about 3 dozen cookies.

Variety: Shape dough into rolls ½ inch thick and 3 inches long or shape into crescents. Bake. Let cool and dust with confectioners' sugar.

Diet: 1–2

BUTTER COOKIES

1 stick (¼ pound) softened   ½ teaspoon baking powder
   butter   1½ cups flour
½ cup sugar   3 tablespoons sweet cream
1 egg yolk   Confectioners' sugar

Preheat oven to 375° F.

Cream butter, sugar, and egg yolk. Add baking powder to flour. Alternate stirring flour and cream into well-beaten butter, sugar, and egg yolk mixture. Mix well until a stiff dough is formed.

Take about a heaping teaspoonful of dough, roll it into a ball, and then between two hands roll into elongated shape and form into crescent. Place crescents on greased cookie sheet and bake for 20 minutes.

Loosen with spatula while still warm but leave cookies on cookie sheet.

When cool, sprinkle with confectioners' sugar.

Makes 20 to 30.

Note: If desired, ½ teaspoon vanilla may be added after egg yolk.

Diet: 1–2

BIG BATCH OF BUTTER COOKIES

½ pound butter or margarine	*3 cups flour, sifted*
1 cup sugar	*1 teaspoon baking powder*
3 eggs	*½ teaspoon baking soda*
1 teaspoon vanilla	

Cream butter and sugar. Add 1 egg at a time, vanilla, and then flour (which has been sifted together with baking powder and baking soda). Wrap in waxed paper and refrigerate overnight.

Preheat oven to 350° F.

Make balls with teaspoon and press down with palm of hand.

Place on *ungreased* cookie sheets and bake for 7 or 8 minutes. When baked, cookies should remain on cookie sheet until cool.

Makes about 200 cookies.

Note: Dough can be kept refrigerated for as long as a week.

Diet: 1-2

CHEESE PASTRY

¼ pound cream cheese   Strained seedless preserves or
½ cup butter, softened   prune butter
1 cup flour

Combine first three ingredients until dough is smooth. Chill.
Preheat oven to 450° F.

When ready to use, roll out dough, as thin as possible, and cut
into 3-inch squares. Put a bit of strained preserves or prune butter
in center of each square. Pick up corners, press together to form
square turnovers. Place on ungreased cookie sheets.

Bake for 15 to 20 minutes. Place sheets on rack and allow cookies
to cool before removing.

Yield: about 24 to 30.

Diet: 1-2

COFFEE BUTTER BITS

1 cup sifted all-purpose flour   1 cup softened butter or
½ cup cornstarch   margarine
½ cup confectioners' sugar
1 tablespoon Sanka instant
   coffee

Sift flour, cornstarch, confectioners' sugar, and instant coffee into mixing bowl. Blend in butter until a soft dough is formed. Chill about 1 hour.

Preheat oven to 300° F.

Shape dough into balls about 1 inch in diameter. Place on ungreased baking sheets, about 1½ inches apart. Flatten with lightly floured fork. Bake about 20 minutes, or until lightly browned. Remove from baking sheets when cool.

Makes about 3 dozen.

Diet: 1–2–3

MERINGUE COOKIES

1 egg white
¼ cup confectioners' sugar
¼ cup granulated sugar

Preheat oven to lowest heat possible.

Beat egg white until stiff. Add confectioners' sugar gradually, constantly beating mixture. Then add granulated sugar in same manner.

Grease a cookie sheet *very* lightly. *Alternate* method is to cover cookie sheet with brown wrapping paper sack.

Take a tablespoonful of batter and with a teaspoon, drop 2 cookies out of each tablespoon onto cookie sheet.

Bake cookies for 1 hour. Do not open oven door before hour is up.

Makes approximately 20.

Variation: Add ¼ teaspoon vanilla.

Diet: 1–2–3

COUNTERFEIT CHOCOLATE (COFFEE FUDGE)

2 cups sugar	1 tablespoon butter
1 cup strong Sanka coffee	⅛ teaspoon salt
1 tablespoon heavy cream	¼ teaspoon cream of tartar

Combine all ingredients in a large aluminum pot, which has been greased with butter only from the edge of the pot to about 2 inches down, to prevent boiling over. Stir with a wooden spoon, over low heat, until sugar is dissolved. Then boil ingredients, quickly, stirring constantly, to the soft ball stage (238° F.). If candy thermometer is not available, this can be tested by dropping a little of the syrup into cold water to see if you can gather it up in your fingers in a soft ball. Remove candy from heat and cool slightly.

Beat with electric mixer, or by hand, until it begins to harden. Then pour onto a greased pie plate. Do not follow the contour of the plate but rather, with the help of a spatula, form a square so that the candy will be about ¾ inch high.

Refrigerate until cold and hard and cut into squares. Makes about 1½ pounds.

Note: This is excellent for appeasing a sweet tooth and is the closest thing I have found to a substitute for chocolate. It should be noted, however, that it should be eaten in *moderation,* by Diet 1 because of the strong coffee and by the other diets because of the high concentration of sugar, which may act as an irritant.

DESSERTS
and Beverages

Because the diet patient is used to being served a great deal of gelatin molds, only a few recipes for these are included. The patient who adores these molds undoubtedly has far more recipes for all the many varieties that are allowed to him than I could collect, so included are only those I found to be a little different from the usual.

My concern was aimed somewhat toward the patient who is a little tired of being served molds constantly, and with these recipes it is hoped that you will have a variety of tasty desserts to soothe a sweet tooth.

In line with this thinking, a few sweet beverages have been included for the patient who was a real soda fountain devotee. Hopefully he will think of these as delicious new concoctions rather than take the negative approach and feel he will have to put up with these substitutes for the fountain creations he used to enjoy.

In a previous chapter the key words of a recipe were discussed. In my opinion the key word for living within the bounds of a diet is *attitude*.

I wish I could guarantee that these recipes will make the patient well. I cannot.

I wish I could say that by adhering to the diet the patient will never again suffer pain or discomfort. I cannot say this either.

I can, however, say that only the patient's *attitude* can govern whether he will abide by the diet, whether he will make an attempt to like, or at least try, foods allowed to him that prior to the diet he had no use for.

With his attitude aimed in the right direction, and this cookbook, his outlook regarding the foods he has been deprived of should improve.

Though this book deals with recipes for people afflicted with gastrointestinal disorders, the idea to compile such recipes was conceived because it was recognized that, regardless of the nature of a person's physical ills, his mental state of well-being is terribly important and cannot be overlooked. Since he cannot survive on, nor be content with, just bread and water, I felt an obligation to utilize his limited diet and make it as palatable as possible.

If this book achieves its goal of making the patient's meals more pleasurable, thus giving him a more cheerful outlook, and if it further keeps even one patient from cheating on his diet and therefore, perhaps, improving his physical condition, this will truly be reward far in excess of the efforts put forth to compile this book.

Diet: 1–2–3

FRUIT SAUCE

1 tablespoon cornstarch
2 tablespoons sugar
¼ teaspoon salt
1 cup fruit juice, as allowed,
   such as juice from canned
   peaches, etc.

1 teaspoon butter or
   margarine

Blend cornstarch with sugar and salt in saucepan. Slowly stir in fruit juice. Cook and stir over medium heat until mixture thickens and boils 2 minutes. Stir in butter or margarine.
Serve hot or cold.
Makes 1 cup.

Note: For sweeter sauce, stir extra sugar into hot cooked sauce until dissolved.
This can be used over all types of desserts, such as puddings, ice cream, etc.

Diet: 1–2–3

APRICOT MOLD

2 *packages (3 ounces each)*	1 *banana*
orange gelatin	1 ✳2½ *can (1 pound 13*
2 *cups boiling water*	*ounces) peeled apricots,*
1 *cup apricot juice*	*preferably in light syrup*

Dissolve gelatin in boiling water and add 1 cup apricot juice from can. If can does not yield a full cup of juice, make up difference with cold water. Put into 6-cup (1½-quart) mold. Mash banana and apricots and add to gelatin after it has thickened slightly. To speed up thickening process, so that fruit may be added, place gelatin in freezer for about 15 to 20 minutes. Refrigerate until firm.
Makes 8 to 10 servings.

Diet: 1–2–3

GELATIN SUPREME

1 package gelatin, any flavor
1 tablespoon to ½ cup ice cream, any flavor—if you are
watching calories, limit ice cream to 1 tablespoon,
otherwise use ½ cup

Make gelatin according to instructions on package. Refrigerate.
When gelatin is partially jelled, put into blender and add ice
cream. Whip and then put into a container and refrigerate.
Add cooked fruit, as allowed on diet, if desired.
Makes 4 to 6 servings.

Diet: 1–2–3

PEACH AND CHEESE SALAD

1 package (3 ounces) cherry   *¾ cup cold water*
  gelatin   *1¼ cups drained canned*
Dash salt   *peaches*
1 cup boiling water   *1½ cups cottage cheese*

Dissolve gelatin and salt in boiling water. Add cold water. Chill
until very thick (about 1½ hours). Fold peaches into 1 cup thickened gelatin. Pour into a 1½-quart ring mold. Chill until set, but
not firm (about additional ½ hour).
Beat cottage cheese until smooth. Whip remaining gelatin until
fluffy. Fold in cheese. Pour into mold over set peach mixture. Chill
until firm and unmold. Center, if desired, can be filled with more
cottage cheese.
Makes 8 to 10 servings.

Diet: 1–2–3

COFFEE SPONGE

1 tablespoon gelatin	*Few grains salt*
2 tablespoons cold water	*3 egg whites, stiffly beaten*
2 cups hot Sanka coffee	*1 cup heavy cream*
2 teaspoons sugar	*1 teaspoon vanilla*

Soak gelatin in cold water and add to hot coffee. Add sugar to taste and a few grains of salt. Strain into a bowl and set in a pan of ice, stirring from bottom and sides. When it begins to thicken, fold in the egg whites.

Turn into a ring mold and set in refrigerator until jelled. Invert onto a chilled platter.

Whip cream until stiff, sweeten to taste and flavor with vanilla, and turn into center of ring.

Makes 6 to 8 servings.

Diet: 1–2–3

COLD BANANA MOUSSE

2½ tablespoons granulated sugar	*2 egg yolks*
1 cup light cream	*2 large ripe bananas*
1 envelope plain gelatin	*1 teaspoon vanilla*
¼ cup milk	*1½ cups heavy cream*

Add granulated sugar to the light cream and scald in the top of a double boiler over boiling water.

Soak the gelatin in the milk.

Beat the egg yolks and gradually add to them a little of the hot cream, stirring constantly. Then add the eggs and cream to the rest of the scalded cream gradually, stirring constantly, and cook until thickened. Remove from fire, add the soaked gelatin, and stir until completely melted. Cool, stirring occasionally.

Meanwhile, peel the bananas, slice them into a large bowl, and crush with a fork or potato masher. Stir in the cooled custard and flavor with vanilla. Beat the heavy cream until very stiff, and fold it into the egg and gelatin mixture. Place in a 1-quart size mold and refrigerate until well set, about 6 hours.

Turn out into a serving dish and serve on cold plates.

Serves 6.

Diet: 1–2

APPLE CHARLOTTE

8 to 12 slices buttered white bread, crusts removed—number of slices depends on dimensions of dish

4 cups canned applesauce

Preheat oven to 450° F.

Line a well-buttered 2-quart baking dish with the slices of buttered white bread, buttered sides of bread touching dish. Fill the dish with 4 cups canned applesauce and cover with more buttered slices of bread, buttered sides up.

Bake until bread is golden brown, approximately 30 minutes, and turn out onto a platter.

Serve warm with heavy cream.

Serves 6.

Diet: 1–2–3

BAKED CUSTARD

3 eggs	*¼ teaspoon salt*
3 cups milk	*1 teaspoon vanilla (optional)*
½ cup sugar	

Preheat oven to 300° F.
Beat eggs slightly. Add milk, sugar, salt, and vanilla (if used). Pour into buttered oven-proof pudding dish or 6 individual custard cups. Set container in a pan with 1 inch of hot water in it.
Bake for 1 hour or until a knife inserted in the custard comes out clean.
Serves 6.

Diet: 1–2

BANANA PUDDING

Substantial quantity of stale sponge cake, cut thin	*Confectioners' sugar*
	Plain Boiled Custard
4 ripe bananas	*1 cup heavy cream, whipped*

Line a deep rectangular dish with stale sponge cake and cover with a layer of sliced bananas. Sprinkle with confectioners' sugar. Repeat, covering with more sponge cake, more sliced bananas, and again sprinkling with confectioners' sugar. Pour boiled custard over bananas and refrigerate for about 1 hour. When ready to serve, cover top with whipped cream.

Plain Boiled Custard

1⅓ cups milk   *2 or 3 egg yolks*
2 tablespoons granulated   *¼ to ½ teaspoon vanilla*
sugar

Heat milk in top of double boiler. Add sugar.
Beat egg yolks until light. Add a little of the hot milk to the
yolks and stir well; then add this to the remainder of the hot milk.
Place over boiling water and cook, stirring constantly, until thickened and until it coats the spoon—about 4 or 5 minutes. Remove
from heat and cool, stirring occasionally. When cold, flavor with
vanilla.
Serves 6.

Diet: 1–2

BREAD PUDDING

6 slices stale bread   *1 teaspoon vanilla (optional)*
1 quart milk   *3 eggs, slightly beaten*
½ cup sugar   *2 tablespoons butter*
½ teaspoon salt

Preheat oven to 325° F.
Trim crusts off bread and cut the slices into cubes. Place bread
cubes into a buttered pudding dish that is oven-proof. Mix together
milk, sugar, salt, vanilla, and beaten eggs and pour over the bread.
Cut butter into small bits and add to the mixture.
Bake 1 hour.
Serve warm or cold with thick cream.
Serves 6.

Diet: 1–2–3

CREAMY RICE PUDDING

⅓ cup rice   ½ teaspoon salt
1 quart milk   ½ cup sugar

Preheat oven to 325° F.
Wash rice well. Put in a sieve and let water run through it.
Butter an oven-proof pudding dish, 2-quart size, and put all ingredients in dish. Bake for 3 hours. Stir several times during first hour to keep rice from settling on bottom.
Serves 6.

Diet: 1–2–3

BAKED BANANAS

Preheat oven to 450° F.
Peel bananas, 1 per person, and place in a buttered baking pan.
Dot with butter and brown sugar and bake for about 15 minutes, until soft and lightly browned.
Serve warm.

Diet: 1–2

DESSERT SOUFFLE

½ *small angel food or*   *1 cup milk*
  sunshine cake, sliced   *1 teaspoon vanilla*
4 eggs

Place slices of cake in a well-greased baking dish. Beat eggs well with the cup of milk and vanilla and pour over cake. Refrigerate overnight.
Preheat oven to 350° F.
One hour before ready to serve: Place baking dish in pan of hot water and bake for 1 hour.
Makes 4 servings.

Diet: 1–2

SURPRISE DESSERT

3 egg whites   *18 Ritz crackers, broken up*
¾ *cup sugar*   ½ *teaspoon vanilla*
½ *teaspoon baking powder*

Preheat oven to 350° F.
Beat egg whites; add sugar and beat until stiff.
Add baking powder, crackers, and vanilla.
Reduce oven heat to 325° F. and bake in a well-buttered glass pie plate for 35 minutes.
Remove from oven and cover with towel while still warm. Cut when chilled.
Makes 6 servings.

Diet: 1–2–3

BANANA MOCHA FROSTED

1 cup milk
1 scoop vanilla ice cream
2 teaspoons Sanka instant
  coffee

2 teaspoons sugar
1 medium banana, peeled
  and chopped

Combine all ingredients in a bowl and beat until well mixed.
Pour into a tall glass.
Makes about 1½ cups.

Diet: 1–2–3

BUTTERSCOTCH FOAM

6 tablespoons butterscotch
  topping
¼ cup half and half

½ pint coffee ice cream
2 cups extra strength chilled
  Sanka coffee

Combine ingredients in electric blender or large bowl of electric
mixer. Blend or beat until frothy.
Serve at once in tall glasses.
Makes 3 to 4 servings.

Diet: 1–2–3

COFFEE-BANANA WHIP

1 banana, peeled   *½ pint coffee ice cream*
1 cup strong Sanka coffee,   *1 teaspoon vanilla*
*   cooled*

Cut banana into chunks. Combine with coffee, ice cream, and vanilla in electric blender. Run blender at high speed until mixture is thick and fluffy.

If banana is puréed first, drink can be made with an electric mixer or hand-operated rotary beater, but it will not be as thick and fluffy as when made in a blender.

Makes 2 servings.

INDEX

Note: The numbers in parentheses which follow each recipe name refer to the Diet Code. Number 1 indicates the Ulcer Diet; Number 2 includes Irritable Digestive Tract, Inflammatory Bowel Disease, and Diverticulitis; Number 3 is the Gluten-free Diet. For more information on the Diet Code, see page xix.